SECRET NATURE

SECRET

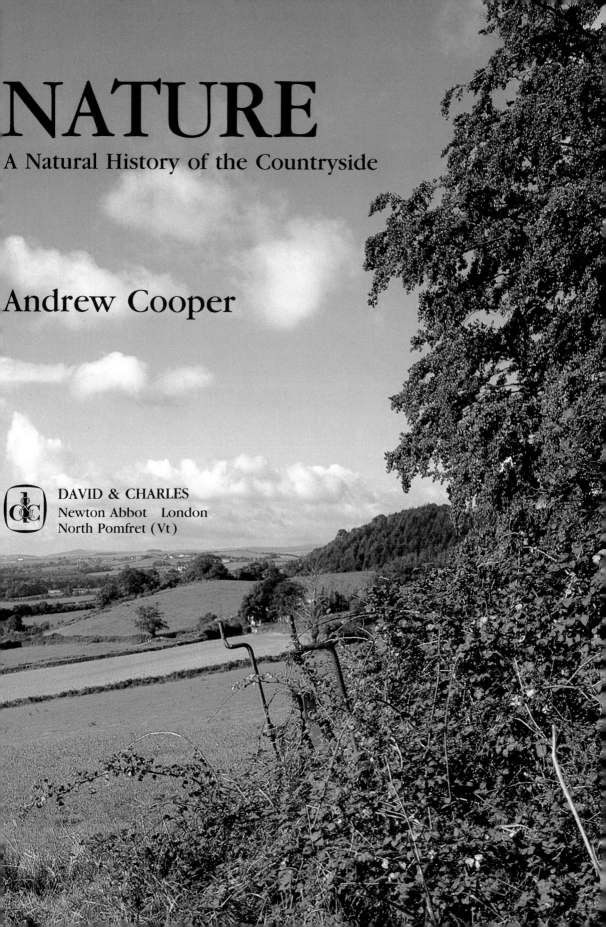

NATURE

A Natural History of the Countryside

Andrew Cooper

DAVID & CHARLES
Newton Abbot   London
North Pomfret (Vt)

To: Jeanne, Julia and Charles

*All photographs taken by the author unless
stated otherwise.*

British Library Cataloguing in Publication Data

Cooper, Andrew, 1951 Feb. 13-
  Secret nature: a natural history of the
  countryside.
  1. Natural history—Great Britain
  I. Title
  574.941   QH137

  ISBN 0-7153-8947-5

Printed in Great Britain
by Butler and Tanner Ltd, Frome
for David & Charles Publishers plc
Brunel House   Newton Abbot   Devon

Published in the United States of America
by David & Charles Inc
North Pomfret   Vermont 05053   USA

CONTENTS

ACKNOWLEDGEMENTS

During the course of filming the series and writing this book I owe a debt of gratitude to many people. To the farmers, naturalists and those working in wildlife conservation who offered their advice so freely, and not least to my colleagues in BBC Television. Especially to David Spires the series executive producer, to editors Justin Smith and Rod Thomas, and to Alison Mills for production assistance. In London my thanks go to Elizabeth Parker for the music, Sebastian Gower-Cliffe for design, and John Kelly and Sheila Hamilton for making the series possible. Last but not least to Mike Read and all at BBC Plymouth for their good humour and sheer professionalism.

Thanks are also due to those without whose assistance many of the photographs would not have been possible, to Roger Hosking whose own superb work also appears in this book and to John Bowers and Wyn Griffiths. I am also indebted to John Cornish, Ellis and Lyn Daw, Peter Barnes, John Robinson, Brian Knox, Noel Allen, Geoff and Gloria Pearson, Tony Flowers, Jemima Parry-Jones and Hubert Snowdon for their help, as well as Lionel, Nick and Nigel Stanbury for allowing me the freedom of their land.

I am most grateful to the scientists who through their research gave me such generous help and advice, in particular to Dr Peter Reynolds, Ian Linn and Elaine Hurrell. For finding so many unusual references and other publications in the course of researching this series, my thanks are due to the librarian and staff of Newton Abbot Library. And for the task of turning my writings into a book I thank David St. John Thomas, Tracey May and David Porteous for their unstinting support and expertise for keeping me on course. I am indeed very grateful to all.

PREFACE

This book is based on a series of wildlife programmes made for BBC television. *Secret Nature* set out to trace the story that is a natural history of the best part of Britain's countryside, a story of people and wildlife in a setting of ancient woods and hedgerows, fields and farms, that began over five thousand years ago and still continues today. A country carved by a pattern of use dictated by centuries of tradition that is quite unlike anywhere else in the world, yet incredibly still retains so much of that original wild legacy from which present day nature descends.

The television series took more than two years in the making and this book was conceived as the filming progressed. It is therefore a companion to the programmes rather than an afterthought, and although originating from the same research the book recalls many of the sights, sounds and events not captured on film. Inevitably only a small proportion of the hours of watching and waiting, travel and learning can be shown on the screen, and so this book is an attempt to redress that balance. For despite the apparently familiar surroundings there were many surprises in store, of drama and delights as well as new and exciting scenes that extended my knowledge of nature – the wildlife that lives alongside man and yet remains hidden for so much of the time.

PROLOGUE

Moaning calls and rising dust greet the morning sun as vast herds of wildebeest move across sun-scorched plains; the clamour of a million pink flamingoes taking to the air or a blizzard of snowgeese descending on the other side of the earth are just a few of the wildlife spectacles to be found worldwide. But the nature of Britain is more subtle, and, although on a totally different scale, can be just as fascinating.

Even in the middle of winter the gently lapping seas off the coast of South Devon maintains a warmth and creates a climate in which sub tropical plants can grow. Yet less than thirty miles away on Dartmoor's windswept tors the conditions are more sub arctic. A microcosm of the country is seen from moor to sea passing through a rural land shaped for the most part by man. The distant call of a cuckoo mingles with the sound of wind blown leaves and songbirds proclaiming their territory. Hedgerows bursting with fresh green growth, walls and banks, and pasture grazed by herds of dairy cattle.

As lowland farms lead on to steeper hills so gently winding rivers turn to rushing streams, and the landscape changes in character. Looking back the countryside stretches far to the distant horizon, a familiar world into which millions of migrant birds pour each spring, and countless insects are born. Mammals hidden deep underground and the watery world of ponds are just some of the subjects that make up the secret nature of the country.

1 INVASION OF THE WILDWOOD

In the half light of gathering dusk, trees and reaching branches take on grotesque new forms; unearthly shrieks and strangling calls, strange shapes and unseen movements in the dark. This is the apparently sinister nature of a woodland experienced at night – no place for modern day man with a fertile imagination. And so it would have seemed to past generations of people living outside the forest. The comfort and security of a fire's flickering flames break the darkness of nocturnal hours in the safety of clearings felled from the surrounding wood.

Today only the world's most primitive people still see nature as benign. Others, and that includes most of us, see the natural world as a malevolent force to be kept at bay from the human race; yet it was not always so. As a new species, mankind at first showed the same extraordinary adaptability as other life forms. The process of evolution gradually resulted in a human frame more closely fitted to its environment, wherever in the world they lived. Man altered slowly over many generations as natural selection produced people of different shapes, sizes and colours – but all variations on the same human theme.

That theme, however, eventually changed its tune with an event first seen in the Middle East, some twelve thousand years ago. In that dry dust-filled atmosphere a rising desert sun would have revealed the dawning of a new way of life. For millenia mankind had lived in small groups, nomadic wanderers, hunting and gathering food as they went. To settle and stay in one place would require an entirely new talent. When confronted by harsh new country no longer would they wait for generations of change while their bodies slowly adapted; they would change their surroundings. Altering the very shape of the land and modifying the plants and animals on which they survived, people began to adapt their world to their own uniquely human needs.

Opposite: Dense deciduous forest today still echoes those ancient wildwoods of the past, with towering trunks, a high canopy of leaves and a tangle of shrubs below. But the wolf and bear have long since gone

The impression of a forest clearing containing an Iron Age settlement is one of the striking images of Butser ancient farm. Fortified by a surrounding ditch and stout palisade of hazel wattled fence the Celtic farmyard appears secure

At around the same time, far to the north and west, the aftermath of the last ice age had left a barren windswept land. Crushed and transformed by the immense weight of vast glacial sheets, western Europe was a wilderness of scattered lakes and bogs left by melting ice. The picture was far from still for, in the land that was to become Britain, the arctic tundra with its herds of reindeer and roaming mammoths, was retreating to the north. Melting ice revealed more land and, along with constantly colonising arctic plants, the tundra moved north in the face of an improving climate.

Longer warmer summers and rising waters had already flooded the Irish channel. And the forests which had spread from the south were still moving northward in the wake of the retreating ice. Beyond the tree line which marked the frontier of the forest, tiny seedlings, no longer killed by the cold, survived. At first, a forest of pine and birch spread across the land, with great thickets of hazel further south. This was no static scene; trees whose seeds were spread not just by the wind but were also carried by jays and squirrels, caused the woodland to advance literally in leaps and bounds.

Flooding meltwater continued to raise sea levels and Britain's land-linking bridge with mainland Europe finally drowned, but not before woodland animals had spread in many successive waves to land reclaimed by the returning forest. As in previous interglacial times, woodland had come and gone in the ebb and flow of ice – now the wood had returned to stay until some future date.

As an island, mainland Britain developed around six thousand years ago beneath a mantle of green – a country cloaked by dense canopies of trees, which stretched as far as the eye could see. Within a thousand years evergreen pine grew mainly in the north along with the seasonal birch. To the south lay an immense wildwood of mixed deciduous trees. Hazel, alder, birch and ash were dominated by towering oak, elm and lime. All but the highest hills were covered in woodland and the only clearings were those on sodden ground – swamps and open water.

The sleek figure of the fox would have slipped through sunlit glades and lurked after dark, while the furry forms of martens hunted higher off the ground. Badgers foraged along well worn paths, much as they do today, and even hares and hedgehogs would have been familiar sights.

The picture of a primeval wood, put together after years of research work, suggests that the romantic image of gigantic trees and a forest echoing to the song of birds may well be close to the truth. This was Britain's final Garden of Eden, the wildwood from which plants and animals descended to modern times. The only difference then to now was the scale of the wood and the unending range of the wild.

It was a time when familiar birdsong would have mixed with some unfamiliar sights – the large predators, lynx, wolf and bear, were then all relatively common. Roe deer browsed the leaves and wild pigs churned the littered log-strewn floor. Beaver and elk lived in the open wooded fringe alongside the lakes, and small bands of people hunted and gathered the life of the forest, just as they had done for thousands of years. Collecting hazelnuts and wild berries they either went in pursuit or trapped for meat.

The red deer was hunted for food and skins as well as antlers, yet was not the largest quarry. The auroch, a massive forerunner of modern cattle, had huge spreading horns and, for people armed only with Stone Age weapons, would have been a formidable prey to tackle. The larger animals might well have been a principal pursuit of early people who outweighed the odds of personal injury against a plentiful supply. Throughout Europe antlers, horns and bones remain as fashioned artefacts of that long lost archaic culture.

Those original Stone Age Britons probably numbered no more than several small tribes and, although living in and around the forest for thousands of years, made little impact on the wood itself and left few clues to their passing. It is not even known when they first arrived. There had been previous nomadic hunters roaming across the tundra, but they had long since moved on as more land was freed from the frozen grip of retreating ice to the north and in front of the advancing pine forests to the south.

Since the coming of the wildwood and settling of the climate to warmer and wetter weather, the forest had remained virtually intact. A natural succession of old trees gave way to clearings after winter gales. Huge trunks lay where they fell and in the void grew fresh growth the following spring. In time clearings were filled and others formed and the wood maintained its natural character, untouched by human hand. That was until five and a half thousand years ago when people of the New Stone Age began to reach these shores.

A Neolithic culture, on the outer edge of a wave of new skills and ingenuity that had begun to spread from the Middle East many years before. They might have been small in stature but not in thought; instead of a wandering life they settled for more permanent ways. The beginnings of a farming tradition had its roots in that remote time from a people with the means to manipulate and fashion the finest of stonework. Razor-sharp flints provided the cutting edge for a new age in which trees fell to the sound of polished stone axes – so began the invasion of the wildwood and the clearance of large tracts of forest. It was to be a transformation from which there would be no turning back. By cutting and clearing, burning and perhaps even ring-barking larger trees, so the newly won land steadily expanded. An increasing population of tribes, along with their cattle and pigs, made remarkable inroads on the surrounding wood.

Elm leaves, browsed by cattle, were an important source of fodder and so not all trees were treated the same. The value of domesticated animals lay as much in their milk and meat as in the trampling of young plant growth. The natural regeneration of the forest would have brought an annual influx of new unwanted seed. But pigs continually disturbed the ground and prevented any chance of wild seedling growth. With the tribes' own seeds of cultivated wheat and herds of cattle and sheep, the expanding open spaces of grassland provided fields for crops and grazing for increasing stock.

The taming of animals by man has a long and often unchartered history. But the dog and pony were probably among the first to be brought under Stone Age control. Herds of goats and sheep had for millenia been managed in the Middle East. And as new types of plants and animals spread slowly from one settlement to another, they eventually reached into Europe – a trade in technology and livestock which at times moved with the pace of a

HELPING HANDS

Of all the creatures that live alongside urban man none is more familiar and encouraged than the red-breasted robin. Perched on the handle of a spade it waits for the turning of the soil as the gardeners earth-filled fork reveals more worms. A close association with a benefit to both – the robin gains access to food and the gardener the plea-sure of wild company. Yet before the coming of people what did the robin do then?

In the more remote parts of Europe where humans are thin on the ground the robin reverts to perhaps its original country companion. The wild boar with its powerful body on short, sturdy legs is well adapted to a nose-grovelling life. Gouging the ground and disturbing the forest floor it goes in pursuit of its habitual preoccupation for roots and fallen acorns. Following along in its wake the resourceful robin picks up the wriggling grubs and worms exposed in the litter. In return an extra pair of ever-alert eyes may well warn the wild boar of any approaching danger.

The Pimperne house at Butser ancient farm is based on evidence from a Dorset excavation. Perhaps a prehistoric manor house, it recreates not only the structure of its building but the atmosphere of an Iron Age dwelling

snail and at others with the speed of the wind. Arriving in Britain, new life brought new ways and the people who adopted the ideas, crops and livestock adapted them, by careful breeding, to improve the selected strains.

While the domestication of sheep and pigs took generations of time and trouble, the taming of the European auroch must have presented a dangerous challenge, if indeed it was ever undertaken. It was a huge animal, even by prehistoric standards, which although ranging widely across Europe since the end of the last ice age, could still be found in the forests of Poland less than four hundred years ago. The last European aurochs disappeared in 1627, long after the last ones in England – which probably did not survive the Bronze Age. From the size of remaining bones and its impressive stance as seen in cave drawings depicted by hunters of an even earlier period, the auroch's image paints a vivid portrait of a powerful beast. Standing up to 2m (6ft) at the shoulder, the bulls were black with a white line running down the spine. Both cows and calves were smaller and reddish-brown in colour.

A few of the earliest domesticated cattle breeds still survive, set aside in special parks and farms. One of the most famous is the Chillingham on the Cheviot Hills. A herd was fenced in during the thirteenth century and although smaller than the original aurochs, the bulls exhibit many wild ancestral traits – they are extremely aggressive towards man. Unlike the dark

15

The power in front of the plough was originally the now long-extinct Celtic shorthorn, which was small but strong and compact with curved, wide-spread horns. The modern day equivalent in size and shape are the long-legged Dexter cattle

coloured aurochs, the Chillingham cattle are almost pure white and this is a feature which appears in many confined herds and flocks. White animals may even have been preferred in the past since such an outstanding colour would have been easier for a herdsman to pick out from the trees. In the wild any genetic freak with such conspicuous markings would be at a distinct disadvantage when compared to the rest of the herd; more easily seen by predators it is doubtful whether it would survive.

The Soay sheep is the last survivor of a prehistoric breed, originating from a Viking-named isle in the Hebrides. Its rams are well known for their aggressive nature despite their small stocky size. And their coarse coats, shaggy and chocolate coloured, often have some buff markings. After several years of confinement in an experimental herd, light spots began to appear. Further work suggests that the original domesticated Soay and other prehistoric sheep could well have been white or at the least, piebald.

A Neolithic landscape would have been impressive, if only for the size of the largest trees – the lime was then common – vast fields cleared of stones and Stone Age man astride a sturdy little pony. Beyond the Neolithic hunter, barking dogs, peacefully grazing sheep and gently rising smoke mark a pointed-roof settlement, enclosed by wattle fencing. Further technology was slow to reach this outpost of people, but when eventually the advantage of metal reached British shores, it took the Neolithic age of stone into one of bronze.

An alloy of Irish copper combined with Cornish tin made a metal tougher than either by itself and this was reflected in the speed of woodland clearance around four thousand years ago. The use of bronze weapons and tools then flourished for a further fifteen hundred years. That was a time when the warm wet weather of the Atlantic period came to an end and the climate became more continental – still warm but very much drier. In the centuries that followed these prolonged dry spells the climate once more became humid and beech trees began to spread across the southern part of Britain.

Bronze, as a metal, had its limitations and the arrival of the Celts with iron, some two thousand five hundred years ago, saw the beginning of the end for the native wildwood. If clearings were large before the coming of the Iron Age, then this new metal enabled Britain's first farmers to make even larger clearings by tackling the denser forests and heaviest of clay soils. Spreading in the wake of these industrious people grassland areas grew rapidly in size. The fields of cultivated corn gently swaying in the wind would then have been a curious sight, for the gold of the ripening grain would have been tinted with the colours of arable weeds – purple corn-cockle, yellow charlock, deep blue gromwell and, one of the most striking of all, the pink yellow cow-wheat. And as if that were not colourful enough, the meadows would have been a brilliant blaze of wild flowers.

Working with iron tools and heavy ploughs which turned the soil changed the profile of the furrowed fields – until that time the wooden ard had dug only a channel. This new way of life was to leave more evidence behind. Reconstructions of ancient settlements today give us a clue to the scale of their building. One of the largest, perhaps a Celtic manor house, used huge straight timbers of oak to support a conical roof of thatch. The weatherproof shelter weighed over sixteen tonnes and that included five tonnes of straw alone. Interlacing hazel rods created walls which were daubed with a mixture of clay and soil – nearly ten tonnes of mud. The entire structure used more than two hundred trees – and that was just for one large house. Far from subsistence farming, recent research has produced some remarkable yields from land farmed using Iron Age methods – perhaps their efficiency and effect was far greater than was at first thought.

Timber was undoubtedly as important in the Iron Age as it was to become during subsequent centuries. Indeed the evidence for tree farming dates back to Neolithic times, when ash, alder and hazel were even then being specially grown. Poles of remarkably similar size were found laid as a timber road across part of the Somerset Levels. Timber of such consistent size could also have been used for hurdles. Around many Iron Age farms the remains of post holes suggest that ancient fields were fenced with hazel.

Originally just part of the wildwood, the importance of hazel to man increased through the ages. A vigorous irrepressible shrub, it was once so common that it is possible the land was covered by vast hazel forests, before the coming of oak. To Stone Age people its nuts were a vital source of food and even a staple item in their diet, while to Irish Druids it was the tree of wisdom and its fruits the food of knowledge. Planted and grown for thousands of years, extensively used for firewood, it might well have been the hazel which fuelled the fires of man's success.

The transformation of the country had affected large parts of Britain and the rolling downs of grassland were as much a feature then as they are now. Close cropped turf and bright blue skies, the summer pastures of Iron Age Britain swayed with a mixed sea of brightly coloured flowers. Skylarks poured their liquid song from above and the sound of Celtic sheep carried on the breeze. It is hard to believe that a population which probably numbered between twenty and thirty thousand people – the size of a single country town today – could have had such a profound effect over so much of Britain.

From small natural glades between the trees, hundreds of grassy acres grew, and domesticated stock continued to suppress the regeneration of the forest, and the numbers of people grew.

When the legions of the Roman empire eventually invaded Britain, far from finding a wild land of trees, they would have discovered in parts a more

The power of the plough to cultivate soil in the past exploited the natural strength of timber with a grown and carved design of the ard. Two cattle-powered and two people were the driving force that began the transformation of the land with a wave of cultivation

gentle pastoral scene. The military mind and Latin organisation, along with efficient ploughs, transformed green pastures into more productive fields of corn and other crops. There were still areas of almost untouched forest but the demand for wood soon consumed more of the remaining trees. Roman Britain was an industrial land where timber was required for military and civil buildings, as fuel for working iron and for heating kilns to fire pottery and brick. Far from continually raiding the wildwood for essential timber supplies the Romans probably developed the smaller wood nearer to hand. Every city and town, army outpost, villa and industrial centre, no doubt had its own coppice of mixed wood. And so the fragmentation of the forest separated by pastures and fields was a pattern set to remain largely unchanged.

When the Roman empire contracted its range, the legions left almost as quickly as they had come. It was to be seven hundred years before the Norman conquest which was the next landmark to affect the natural history of what was now a farming country. In the early years which followed the Roman void, people reverted to a more basic way of life and the pace of woodland clearance came virtually to a halt.

The Dark Ages left little historical evidence and by now the last of the giant aurochs had gone from their final Scottish domain. Wolves and bears still roamed the wilder parts but they, too, were under threat. The carpentry skills of Anglo Saxon people ensured the continuity of coppiced wood. Timber-framed houses rather than ones of stone, as well as an increasing demand for shipbuilding, took a never-ending toll on the wildwood's mature trees. Wooded pasture opened up still more grazing and the spread of these parklands with their large scattered trees, began to move north. Villages appeared throughout the length and breadth of the land and Christian churches, with local economies, established many of their present known names.

Some animals and plants suffered as a result of woodland destruction, while others benefitted from increasing new ground. That most ubiquitous of all small birds, the house sparrow, followed man's agricultural success. Nesting in and around buildings, feeding on spilt grain, its numbers increased and it spread. Perhaps it owed its success as much to the availability of food as to its shy nature – despite an apparent tameness the sparrow maintains a wary suspicion of man.

Screaming swifts on scimitar wings scything through the air in pursuit of insect prey, would have been a familiar sight and sound, even in Neolithic summer days. The swallow, too, is attracted by swarming flies following herds of cattle – a convenient and reliable seasonal source for its flying food. Both these birds were once confined to nesting in caves or perhaps under larger birds' nests. They are seldom, if ever, seen in woodland and so would have been rare before the coming of the first farmers. Living in the shadow of man and nesting in his buildings gave these fast flying migratory birds a new lease of life.

Hazel was an important part of rural life in the past as its strength and pliability made it an asset interwoven with countrycrafts. Not least was its use in thatching to hold in place the roofs that kept generations of people dry

House martins were essentially cliff nesters and along with cave dwelling swifts and swallows, their natural sites must have been few and far between. Thatched roof dwellings followed by more substantial buildings of stone flourished in Roman times and perhaps provided the first artificial cliffs, tucked up under the shelter of a Roman roof. But it is only in comparatively recent years that the house martin has spread so widely.

Birds were not the only creatures to move in with man, for wherever he set up home so too did the mouse. The house mouse is an opportunist which reached these shores the same way as the first Celtic farmers – by boat. Hidden amongst cargoes of grain and seed, the mouse would have been carried with man from home to home.

But far more important than this little rodent, in terms of carrying disease, was its larger black relative, the rat. Once thought to have spread across Europe in medieval times, it is now known to have invaded Britain along with the Roman army. Its success of spreading by sea earned it the name of 'ship rat', and it is quite distinct from its cousin the brown rat, which did not reach Britain until the latter part of the seventeenth century. Recorded outbreaks of unknown pestilence and plague litter the pages of history, long before the tragedy of the Black Death. The disease was transmitted by fleas and, carried by black rats, it spread amongst the steadily growing

20

settlements. As towns grew into cities the rising tide of fleas and lice, bedbugs and mites pestered and plagued the life of Roman soldiers and servants alike. Is it any wonder that mankind considered the wild world of biting, scratching and sucking hordes to be anything but benign?

The year 1066 brought the Norman invasion and William to a pastoral land still scattered with trees, but records from the Domesday Book revealed a chronic shortage of timber. Set aside by regal command royal forests were established and controlled by punitive laws, for the care of the wood and protection of its game. Though the Norman concern for trees probably reflected their passion for hunting, as much as a valuable resource for building, and as such the royal forests flourished under their rule.

Small areas of wildwood which had escaped the onslaught of previous centuries, surrounded by planted trees, were spared the woodsman's axe. Much of the wildlife which remained came under increasing threat, as some species had already been hunted close to the point of extinction. Just when certain animals eventually disappeared is often hard to tell but as the lynx has no Celtic or Old English name, it is thought to have gone the way of Stone Age man – without descendants.

The largest predator of all, with a popular notorious image to match its immense size, is the European brown bear. Its reputation as an aggressive

Stone is far more durable than wood and began to supersede timber buildings in Romano-British times. Based on excavations this house is thought to be a grain drier, but its real purpose perhaps still lies buried with its original remains

BUTSER ANCIENT FARM

Some two and a quarter thousand years ago in the second century BC the Chinese were building the Great Wall, at about the same time that the Greek mathematician Archimedes was pondering the principles of physical laws. Back in Britain the Iron Age had seen the construction of hill top forts, thatched roof-villages, and the continued clearance of forest with the growth of the farm.

Today the remains of past civilisations survive either in stone or inscription, providing a tangible link with an age and way of life that sowed the seeds for the present generation. In Britain monuments to that time are carved in the hills, yet the scale and extent of massive earthworks only becomes apparent where you can walk between the weathered and grass covered ramparts. The defence of a culture that eventually crumbled with the advance of the Roman invasion.

But fortifications were only part of the picture of life in those times and today little remains of their houses and existence. Digging back into the past often revealed only post holes and tantalising clues to their lifestyle, and so the reconstruction of an Iron Age village based on actual evidence, was a valuable tool that gave the researchers chance for further work – a unique project in the world of archaeology that anyone can look around.

For the first time a long term trial of farming techniques could yield information so long denied to others working in that field.

Ploughs and arable tools accurately remade are used to cultivate the land for the sowing of old fashioned crops, later to be harvested and stored according to the custom of the day. Oxen, pigs and primitive sheep all add to this living portrait of Iron Age farm life built on the grounds of an original prehistoric site.

Within the walls of the largest house entire hewn trees rise into the vaulted roof, where smoke from a central fire lingers under the straw thatch. Shadows dancing on stretched animal skins and the sound of distant sheep create an atmosphere transported from a different time. As a measure of celtic life the Butser ancient farm project has earned modern respect for a tough yet in their own way, a highly civilised people.

carnivorous beast probably bolstered the credit for bravery of those who hunted it, rather than revealing the facts. The truth is far less spectacular. The brown bear is mainly vegetarian, feeding on nuts and berries as well as large quantities of grass. In addition it will add ants and voles to a surprisingly omnivorous diet. Generally docile by nature a female may well live up to its ferocious reputation, when in defence of its young. Wandering widely in search of food, bears tend to keep very much to themselves, well away from man. After hibernating during winter it is in early spring that bears, driven by hunger, could be compelled to turn carnivorous, especially where natural food supplies have been reduced by human encroachment onto wild land. Bears might then attack farm stock or the young of wild boar or deer, but where still common in the more remote parts of Europe, with plentiful food, bears have been seen peacefully foraging amongst herds of cattle and sheep.

Indeed, so common were bears in Roman Britain that they were caught and transported to the Imperial Circus in Rome. Even until Norman times bears appeared to have survived, yet by the end of that century they had all but disappeared from Britain.

In a cold bleak outpost, far from their native land, invading Roman troops would have huddled around the warming flames of a fire. It was a wretched life in this far-flung corner of their empire made miserable as much by awful weather, as by the eerie howling from high in the hills – the cry of the wolf. Nine hundred years later records reveal that the wolf was still common enough in Britain, and keeping the wolf from the door was a full-time occupation for many people in the past – defending their flocks of sheep. The subject of folklore and legend, these distant ancestors of dogs seemed to obsess and terrorise townsfolk and countrymen of the time. In England the wolf was driven to extinction early in the fifteen hundreds, only managing to survive in Scotland by literally taking to the hills. Legend then tells of the last wolf killed in the Highlands – the year was 1743.

Whether by accident or design, both the beaver and wild boar went the way of the wolf many years before, hunted into extinction by the excesses of the human predator. Yet this was nothing new – it is not beyond the bounds of possibility that hunting had exterminated other species in the past. The elk and giant deer, even mammoths and woolly rhinoceros perhaps fell to well aimed Stone Age spears and cleverly designed traps. Apart from the auroch, beaver and boar, wolf and wild bear, no other native mammal has become extinct in Britain for well over two thousand years.

The pattern of land use was given order and new impetus under Norman command. The hazel copse, organised on a seven year cycle of coppicing and growth, exploited the pliable nature and considerable strength of this valuable long-used crop. A material increasingly in demand for fencing, thatching spars, tool handles and faggots for the fire, all came from the carefully coppiced wood.

Production from the land increased and, as trade became established, an interconnecting network of roads and lanes came into considerable use. The

23

Normans also brought in new animals and, besides reintroducing the pheasant after the Romans had gone, they introduced a Mediterranean mammal to be bred for fur and flesh — the rabbit had arrived. At first the animals were kept and maintained in purpose-built warrens, far too valuable for release into the wild. But the inevitable escapes occurred and the burrowing hordes found a country ripe for the eating.

From the coming of William the Conqueror, the feudal lands of England were controlled by a harsh manorial system which lasted for more than two centuries. Its end was brought about by an invasion of a more insidious kind. A major catastrophe unleashed on medieval times was to have far-reaching effects on the countryside. The incidence of pestilence rose to plague proportions in 1348, spread by increasing numbers of black rats. Continual sporadic outbreaks of this virulent disease culminated in the horror of the Black Death — and the great bubonic plague which erupted in 1665.

The coming of the Celts to the beginnings of the plague was a period spanned by less than ninety human generations, yet in less than one generation the population was cut by a third. It struck most severely in town slums and country hovels the people who worked the land. The labour force was savagely reduced. Entire families and village populations died in the cruel trail of this terrible disease and the consequences for the country were no less dramatic.

Fields remained untilled and coppices overgrown, cottages and whole hamlets were left derelict and deserted, slowly crumbling into the soil in a rising sea of scrub. Medieval farm life came grindingly to a halt and the shortage of labour left thousands of acres untouched. Around abandoned settlements wild flowers bloomed unchecked. At first a total lack of disturbance saw woodland and heath regaining lost ground. The silence in the aftermath of death broke with the rising crescendo of birdsong and an explosion of animal life. Nature moved in where people once lived. It was a temporary reprieve for the wildwood which returned to previously cultivated land with a germinating wave of trees and shrubs.

Despite the devastation of those first few decades some farms survived but a change had taken place. The need for easier, less labour-intensive exploitation of the land brought a returning tide of sheep nibbling back the forest, and pasture was here to stay. The invasion and subsequent surrender of the ancient wildwood was by now all but complete. Managed and manipulated for millenia, most of the wood that remained had lost its native character and yet surprisingly had retained much of its original wildlife.

In Elizabethan England the need for mature and shapely oak grew with a demand for fighting ships, the galleons of the naval fleet. Charcoal burning

Opposite: Wooden fences woven from coppiced hazel branches were no doubt the original walls that divided man from nature. As field boundary and wattled foundation for mud-daubed buildings, the hazel has been used from prehistory to present day

also grew as the needs for smelting heat increased with the manufacture of cannons, anchors and chains, along with hand weapons and tools. Where large timber was required individual trees were remembered and watched, marked down for a purpose twenty or thirty years hence. Smaller but no less useful trees, then planted round about, gave rise to the traditional growth of coppice with standards.

The first arable fields laid out by early Anglo Saxons used only the best ground, but an increasing population required increasing food yields and more but poorer lands were enclosed by Elizabethan farms. The open fields of village life became increasingly threatened and landless peasants migrated en masse into the towns. The urban growth put greater pressure on the land available for food, as well as on wild animals and plants.

Food shortages and half-starved populations fed the spreading plague. It was an attitude of the time which preferred fields of grazing sheep for wool to crops for human consumption. Sheep, however, constantly left their contribution to the land, with the subsequent improvement in its fertility.

The descendants of the dispossessed and landless peasants created a work force which fueled the Industrial Revolution. The backbone of urban life became the ruling class in the towns, dictating terms for improvement of their own and rural life. New laws enclosed more land and, in the three hundred years up to 1939, began another revolution – but this time down on the farm.

The face of Britain was changing yet again and England, especially, became a country crisscrossed by miles of hedgerow, which on stony ground gave way to walls. Some counties managed to retain a survivor from the past, open common ground for grazing, surrounded by a patchwork of fields. The hedgerow became a feature in places such as Devon, where in 1844 a survey of just ten parishes by John Grant found 1,651 miles of hedge – 'a length half as long again as the great wall of China'. The entire county must then have contained up to 60,000 miles of hedgerows and banks, bursting with wild flowers.

Whether dug and planted, or carved from a wood when cleared, one of the greatest manmade habitats must have run for uncountable miles. And of all the hedgerow trees the one that was used the most was the hawthorn. Planted from cuttings, its fast densely-branched growth, armed with cattle deterring thorns, was used to good effect. Producing a strong hedge in the minimum of time earned it its country name – 'quickthorn'.

In time the arrival of wild seeds would have added other trees and shrubs – blackthorn, elder, crabapple and scrambling wild roses – a growing structure that would have gained in intertwining strength. After ten years or so the top was slashed and laid, creating a remarkably impenetrable barrier. Elm was often encouraged as a valuable fodder for cattle and ash was allowed to grow. Even the holly was left alone – but more out of superstition than with an eye for future wood – it was considered unlucky to cut down a holly tree.

THE FIRST FARMLAND

Crowned with a beechwood copse, rounded slopes and springy turf, valleys where no streams run, and the scattered white outcrops of dug chalk are nowhere but the downs. Shallow soiled and easily drained, the once well wooded rising lands of southern England still retain traces of field systems, made by pre-historic man. Flints mined from chalk for weapons and tools eventually gave way to metals. Cultures that left more than their mark on the land, in the shape of gigantic figures and tracks etched in the ground, seeded a way of life.

Yet other parts of the country also lay claim to ancient settlements and long established patterns of use. Far from east coast invasions, seats of power and political unrest, the west country has seen farmland flourish for millenia. It is the soil and shape of the underlying ground that dictates the agricultural scheme as much as the climate, and generations then followed tradition. Houses built according to the lie of the land, crops grown and stock reared that thrived in the prevailing conditions, produced the variety and wealth of the countryside.

Apart from dividing fields, hedgerows formed a boundary to an irregular network of dirt roads and narrow muddy lanes. Highways and byways, as far removed in time from the purpose-planned and engineered system of Roman roads as they were in their basic design, and were not so much built as following centuries of traditional use.

With the clearance of so much woodland, both archaic and comparatively new, the importance of hedgerows for wildlife has steadily grown. A linear extension of the forest, spreading out into the farm, it is a living corridor connecting dwindling woods – a lifeline from the past for forest dwellers. Many plants, such as bluebells and dog's mercury, remain as relics of woodland long since gone. In the oldest hedgerows more than five hundred species of plants have been found. They in turn attract a multitude of insects which then draws in the mammals and birds. Some of the oldest hedgerows today are a living legacy of Britain's first farmers, a poignant reminder of, and tangible link with the past.

From primeval pools to the farmer's pond, the need for pure, fresh water is as great for livestock, as it is for wildlife. In winter, streams bubble and gurgle with the flow of cold water, while in summer they may dry to a trickle. So man in his ingenious way dammed and impeded their paths and the ponds so created ensured a constant supply of year-round fresh water.

Ponds were lined with an impermeable layer of clay, or cobbled down one side, and here the life of the farm could come to drink and wash. Sometimes they were built close to a yard for shire horses to be washed down, others were built at the junction of two or three fields.

Newly dug ponds are soon colonised by aquatic forms of life. The seeds and leaves of various waterweeds might well have flown in from afar – carried on the feet of ducks and other waterbirds. Even toads moving from pond to pond can transport bits of plants on their backs – duckweed can arrive this way. Windblown, walking or flying in, the life of the pond increases as the seasons go by. But continually trampled by cattle and sheep coming down to drink, few plants can grow around its margins. Only on the steeper banks can willow and alder trees gain a deep-rooted hold.

Steam brought new sounds and power to the pace of life on the land. Threshing machines turned by traction engines appeared at the beginning of the agricultural revolution, and travelled from farm to farm

With the advent of steam the farming revolution got underway. There followed a period of intensive mechanisation that was to reach far into farm life. Powerful engines drove threshing machines and even began to pull ploughs. For the first time in the history of the land the pace of work was no longer dictated by the speed of oxen or horses. And the destruction of many wild parts was carried out in the interests of agricultural gain. From the seventeenth century until the arrival of machines, the speed of change gathered momentum. Unable to adapt to the quickening pace wildlife suffered unprecedented loss.

The farmers whose ancestors had continued the creation of the countryside were to witness a new generation, driven in pursuit of profit at the expense of the natural life of the land. Specialisation produced crops grown only in the best conditions rather than where they were needed – resulting in the monoculture typical of eastern counties. But of all the inventions of man the shotgun was to have a profound effect on the course of the country's natural history. A mass extermination of any creature sharp in tooth, beak or claw, began in the name of game protection – predators great and small all fell to the blast of the gun or were ensnared in lethal traps.

Yet nature still survived just as it had in Norman forests left for the hunt, so corners of the country remained wild and virtually untouched. From the very earliest beginnings in that remote Iron Age and beyond, the countryside had changed at each historical landmark; a journey in time that spans five thousand years from ancient wildwood to the modern farm. Slowly, a random pattern of woods and fields, hedgerows and ponds emerged. And with it there evolved a unique mix and diversity of life, unlike any other country in the world.

For all the upheaval and destruction, laws, famine and plague, the beauty that is Britain's green and pleasant land grew in the wake of a farming tradition. Despite the few casualties on the way, as well as new introductions, the nature of the countryside has survived surprisingly intact.

Casting lengthening shadows across autumn fields, the evening light throws freshly furrowed soil into sharp relief. Above the green valley of a well kept farm, the rusted iron shape of an old seed drill lies rotting in a hedge. Stirring the scene, a breeze sends a final flurry of copper coloured leaves tumbling from a lonely beech. The weatherworn handles of the old implement have served for many years, both as a reminder to man of those first mechanised days and as a perch for generations of resident robins. As the sun follows its path into distant hills, the ruffled rounded wings of a cock pheasant lift it noisily onto the iron perch. An alien bird, now living in the wild, stands on a discarded tool in a hedge dug and planted by human hand – for all its apparent naturalness the countryside today is essentially manmade.

Still surviving in a corner of the country is the binder that produced ready-tied sheaves of corn. The design was simply modified as the days of horse-drawn implements were numbered, first by steam and then by the increased power and potential of petrol-driven tractors

TREES IN TIME

There is nothing more impressive in life than standing beneath the towering stature of a tall tree, with wide spreading branches reaching out into the sky. Self supporting, only bending before the fury of a gale, its sheer size dwarfing all other plants and animals around.

Since people first felled forests, trees have held an importance in cultural economy, an essential ingredient for construction; man and wood have gone hand in hand down through the ages. Whether as weapons of war or in defence of homelands, tools of a trade or the structure of ships, timber not only supported the fabric of society but gave greater mobility with the invention of the wheel. Sitting upon wooden chairs kings have ruled the land that was at first kept clear by the use of the original plough, the ard had no metal parts.

The fruits and leaves of some trees are edible to man and beast, while others are poisonous to people, yet all have a value in the nature of life. As landmarks or tied to historical events trees not only create the more recent pages that actually make up the history books, but feature large in its text.

Certain trees are incredibly long lived with their roots stretching far back in time. The age of a few trees are known from the date of their planting, or historical associations, and indelible proof is described by its growth in the form of annual rings. The counting of a section one first learns as a child, is a destructive method for recording a result, literally stopping the trees in its tracts. In contrast a modern development for dating a tree leaves it still standing and unharmed, by taking a core drilled from its trunk and refilling the hole to prevent any rot.

Some of the largest and a few of the oldest oaks are linked in legend to the days of Robin Hood, and may well have been growing at that time. Five hundred years is not unusual for these trees and some may be considerably older. One of the oldest are coppiced stools, the base of an ash that is self renewing and perhaps capable of living indefinitely. The counting of rings that tell not only the variety of growing conditions reflecting the vagaries of the climate, but when and at what intervals the coppice was cut back. One very large base in West Suffolk could be at least a thousand years old and still growing a good crop of ash poles.

But the oldest surviving single tree is one of a long lived species. An evergreen yew in a churchyard near the shores of Loch Tay in Perthshire is reputed to be over 1,500 years old, and still bearing a large and healthy green crown. A living plant just two trees from prehistory.

Britain		Rest of the World
Aftermath of the ice age, tundra with pine and birch forest in the South.	c.9700BC	Cultivated crops grown in Thailand.
Broad leaved trees spreading North.	c.8000BC	Wheat cultivated in Middle East and domesticated animals begin farming settlements.
Britain still part of mainland Europe inhabited by stone age hunters.	c.6700BC	Evidence of 14 different crops grown in Southern Turkey.
Warming climate and rising seas, vast forests and Britain becomes an island.	c.6000BC	Beginning of rice growing in Far East.
	c.5000BC	Maize cultivated in Mexico.
Farming begins in Neolithic Britain.	c.4000BC	Wheel used in Mesopotamia.
Elm tree decline perhaps linked to land clearance.	c.3000BC	Plough being used in Middle East.
Lynx probably extinct.	c.2700BC	Age of pyramids in Egypt begins.
Wessex culture develops in Bronze Age Britain, the builders of Avebury and Stonehenge.	c.2000BC	Minoan and Mycenean civilisations build in Crete and Greece.
Large scale land clearance makes major inroads into wildwood.	c.1500BC	Egyptians harness oxen to the plough.
Hill top settlements built in the south of the country.	c.1300BC	Hittite civilisation in Mesopotamia discover iron smelting.

Britain		Rest of the World
Celtic people invade.	c.1000BC	The siege of Troy.
The Iron age reaches Britain and hill forts massively reinforced.	c.500BC	Greek and Phoenician civilisations colonise Mediterranean.
Auroch probably extinct in England and Wales.	c.300BC	Roman Empire expanding.
Belgic immigration begins and introduces heavy oxen-pulled plough.	c.120BC	House mouse probably spread across Europe.
	c.AD30	Jesus crucified and Christianity founded.
Roman invasion of Britain.	43	
Main withdrawal of Roman troops begins.	383	Mayan civilisation begins in Central America.
Angles, Saxons and Jutes establish settlements.	c.400	The sack of Rome.
Auroch perhaps finally extinct in Scotland and Brown Bear in Britain.	c.1000	Black rat spreads from continent into Britain.
Norman conquest.	1066	Greenland vikings reach America.
Domesday survey.	1086	
Beaver extinct.	c.1100	First crusade.
First record of rabbit in British Isles.	1176	
Land enclosures begin.	1235	
	1347	Black Death spreads across Europe.
Black Death in England.	1348	
Wolf probably extinct in England.	1492	Columbus reaches America.
Wild boar probably already extinct.	1620	Mayflower puritans settle in New England.
The Great Plague.	1665	
Brown rat arrives.	c.1728	Jethro Tull the agricultural machine inventor travels the continent for ideas to improve British farming.
Wolf finally extinct.	1743	
Harvest mouse first described by Gilbert White.	1785	
Red squirrel decline and grey squirrel introduced.	c.1900	
Farm labour reduced by war in Europe.	1914	Outbreak of World War I.
Vast areas turned over to crop production.	1939	Outbreak of World War II.

2 A NATURAL HISTORY OF THE FARM

Threatening grey clouds stream overhead as gale force winds and torrential rain lash the farm. Trees bend and barns whistle, adding to the deafening roar as a spring storm tears at the land. Darkness comes early with such bad weather and the howling continues into the night.

Waking in the small hours of dawn something has stirred you from your sleep, but there is not a sound – the gale has passed. Morning brings a transformation to yesterday's scene, calm clear air and bright blue skies. Drying rays from the sun have transformed the rain-soaked farmhouse thatch into gently rising clouds of steam. Chickens cluck and pigeons coo – the farm, sheltered at the head of a coombe between rolling green hills in the heart of Devon, has weathered yet another storm.

For perhaps a thousand years there have been buildings on this very site and the land had probably been tilled even long before that. Such is the ancient nature of some of the oldest farms. For over two thousand years people have laboured and ploughed, dug and planted, reaped and stored the produce of the land. There are parts of the West Country that claim to have the oldest established pattern of agriculture in the country. Yet the history of the land and its wildlife goes back far beyond these. In the brief span of one hundred and fifty human generations, three thousand years, the face of Britain has changed from the depths of an enclosing forest to the open space of the farm.

An idyllic rural picture conjures up the image of a traditional farm. The locality mentioned in the Domesday Book has ancient weathered buildings, with thatched roof and old exposed beams, lichen covered solid stone walls, and a range of equally antique barns and outbuildings all clustered round a cobbled yard. The sounds of chickens scratching for spilt grain competing with flocks of sparrows and a garden full of cottage flowers buzzing with the contented hum of insect life. Beyond the house lies an old orchard with the first signs of pink blossom bursting from bright green buds. But sadly this is a scene rapidly becoming more fantasy than fact as many old farmhouses have been pulled down and others sold off to the encroaching towns. In the past

Opposite: Like an island refuge in a sea of corn an old barn lingers on. A reminder of past hay-making days, and now seldom disturbed, its importance for wildlife over the years has grown with its decline

32

invading armies and new cultures brought about the greatest changes. But in recent years the most dramatic events have been wrought by big business, streamlining traditional farms.

There are, however, still corners of the countryside which remain remarkably untouched – while others have, unfortunately, compromised generations of tradition for an easier and more profitable life on the land. But where farming traditions continue with a practised eye and knowledge of natural life, the nature of the countryside can still survive and even thrive. By today's standards our Bronze and Iron Age ancestors were not efficient farmers. Cleared woodland produced fields which grew only a few seasons' crops, before impoverished soil forced a move to newly felled ground. In contrast, the twentieth-century landscape is a surprisingly stable scene.

When Britain first became an island the vast majority of wild plants formed the forest itself where most of the animals also lived. Freshwater, mountain and moorland species added to the inland native list, and in the intervening years there have been only some losses but also huge gains. No less than a third of the country's current floral list consists of introduced plants – some seven hundred species in all.

Whether accidental garden escapes now living and seeding wild or purposely introduced, many plants are now accepted as a permanent part of the countrywide scene. Some of the largest and most familiar trees are relatively new to Britain – the sycamore, known from the late sixteenth century, became a fashionable planting on the nobleman's estates. Originally from southern and central Europe it now far outnumbers its native relation, the field maple.

From east of Italy in the Balkans came the horsechestnut, renowned amongst generations of boys for its hard wearing nut – the conker. It was planted in avenues on roadsides or around the larger country estates just like the larch, which until the middle of the seventeen hundreds was considered purely a decorative tree. Only in recent times have landowners realised the potential for a timber harvest from a hybrid of Japanese and European larch. Resistant to both exposure and disease its light shade was an added bonus, not spoiling areas set aside for rough shooting.

Cultivated acres of exotica today cover much of lowland Britain – arable crops, barley, wheat, beet and potatoes are the most common, and many grass leys containing few native plants. An ebbing woodland tide over past millenia opened up vast new areas to increasing numbers of arable weeds. Cornfields once glowed red with acres of poppies while others reflected the bright yellow sun with a golden garden of corn marigold. Throughout the summer months a successive sea of wildflowers gave a natural display of spectacular colour. The heyday for flowers in the fields passed with the coming of modern and more refined agricultural techniques. Efficient seed cleaning and chemical sprays kept at bay or killed the majority of arable weeds, which for some was a practical necessity as many of these plants could taint or even add poison to the crop. Of all wild flowers which pervaded the crops of the past the field cow-wheat was one of the most beautiful. Now a rarity in itself it was once the scourge of farmers, as its size and shape is so similar to the wheat seed. Yet seen in historical terms many of these arable weeds are today as rare as they once were, when the country was covered with trees.

Without the benefit of hindsight past generations of people were unaware of the consequences of alien introduction to the wild, and brought in many new animals to enliven their scene. The novelty and beauty of the North American grey squirrel made for its popular release in gardens and parks. The first to arrive came from the eastern states around 1876. Over the following years several introductions took place but not until 1889 were the first well documented releases made. A present from an American visitor to the Duke of Bedford, these were given their freedom in Woburn park. Again two years later, a further ten squirrels were released and by the turn of the century their numbers were naturally increasing and many more were given away – an acceptable gift of the day. Within fifty-five years some thirty-two separate introductions were recorded. But by the time a law prohibiting further releases was passed in 1937, the grey squirrel was well on its way to colonising entire parts of the country.

By any standards it was a spectacular spread, unhindered by competition

The sight of red poppies growing in the corn was once a regular sight, but today is considered to be bad farming practise and as such is controlled by seed cleaning and herbicidal sprays on the majority of farms

or predators. At the time of the original releases the native red squirrel had already declined, possibly decimated by disease, and only owls and foxes could prey on weak or young grey squirrels. Even today dogs, cats and cars are thought to take the heaviest natural toll, besides the numbers killed for damaging forestry plantations – their appeal belying their destructive nature.

Another introduced rodent is also an unwelcome but firmly entrenched part of the farm, an opportunist that was accidently brought in by man – the brown rat is no friend of the farmer. Spreading from Asia through Russia to the west, they are thought to have begun their sea-borne invasion of Britain in the early seventeen hundreds. In contrast to the mainly urban dwelling and building inhabiting black rat, the brown is far more adaptable. Equally at home in sewers, earthbanks and barns as well as out and around the fields, in less than a century the brown had replaced the black as the most common British rat.

Rodents are not the only latterday successes in mammalian migration to spread across the country. One of the most persistently voracious predators, probably whose only redeeming feature is to prey on rats, is the North American mink. A capable climber and swimmer this larger relative of weasel and stoat was originally just bred for its fur. In the years following World War II escapes were reported from a Lancashire breeder. The first indication of a new alien on the loose came after it had caused considerable depradation in nearby poultry farms. But these initial reports soon came to an end and it was assumed the mink had failed to become established. 1953 was to be the turning point for the main invasion of the mink. From the picturesque Teign valley in Devon came waterbailiff reports of a decline in rats and increasing sightings of mink, the result of a series of escapes from a Bovey Tracey farm which had closed about the same time. Moving up the Teign river to the moorland watersheds the animals spread by following other West Country streams. Since then the mink has appeared in the wild all across the country as further escapes added to their increasing population – from Penzance to Perthshire the mink has carved its predatory niche.

Joining the ranks of the released and accidental introductions, the mink is only one of a long line of foreign animals now living and breeding in the wild. Of the sixty-seven terrestrial mammals as many as twenty-seven are not regarded as strictly native. Norman rabbits and Japanese deer, American squirrels and Asian rats and mice, these are but a few of the world's fauna which found a new home in Britain.

Some of the most obvious and perhaps even welcome additions to the native lists have been the avian arrivals – fancy ducks and elegant geese released on ornamental ponds, and strutting amongst the shrubs, a colourful

Opposite: A brilliant massed display of corn marigolds growing in wild abandonment carpet an old field, and are a colourful reminder of the flowers which were once a common sight. Modern seed cleaning, as much as chemicals, have reduced arable weeds

array of golden, aristocratic and Chinese pheasants. It was also from the east that one of the most spectacular successes of the avian kind came. Arriving with the speed of the wind it took the Asiatic collared dove just ten years to take Britain by storm. From birdwatchers' books and nesting records in 1955 its colonisation of farms and villages, country towns and gardens has been recorded as one of the most dramatic natural events seen this century. The British extension of its range was but another small step in its trans-European explosion. Travelling from Turkey and the Balkans to British shores in less than twenty years, the population of this diminutive dove has expanded and increased in a remarkable way.

Far less spectacular yet on its own a similar story of success, was the introduction and subsequent spread of the little owl. Today it is a typical bird of farmland with its buoyant bounding flight, large yellow eyes and fierce little expression. Since it was first imported by an eccentric squire in 1842, to subsequent releases by other people into the next century, the little owl became a permanent visitor and regular sight around certain farms. But during the nineteen thirties, at the height of its English expansion, it aroused the unwelcome and ill-informed attention of land-owners and keepers. Accused of taking game chicks, the little owl became the subject of a special commissioned enquiry. In the absence of any real proof it was tried and sentenced in letters to the press. But in its defence the evidence from thousands of regurgitated food pellets revealed its largely insectivorous diet. Acquitted and freed from persecution the little owl's continued increase can still be seen today.

Arriving by air or sea, the flying and swimming species were not barred when Britain became an island. Yet for the crawling, hopping and wriggling species the land bridge with continental Europe was the final point of entry. From the end of the last ice age to conditions warm enough for amphibians and reptiles to survive, probably left less than two thousand years for the arrival of a small variety of frogs and toads, newts, lizards and snakes.

By far the greatest in terms of both number and diversity of form are the seemingly infinite hordes of insect life. Since Stone Age man first swatted mosquitoes and flies, to the farmer's agrochemical arsenal, insects have been a mixed blessing to anyone who works the land – from beneficial bees to the constant consumers of crops, farmers have battled for centuries against the odds. But today with an array of lethal insecticides to combat any persistent pest and herbicides to control unwanted weeds, man has the means to destroy on a vast scale.

On farmland perhaps more than any other place, wildlife does not flourish without the consent and co-operation of the farmer. Since man first farmed the structure of our wildlife has probably been governed, not so much by nature, but more by the plants and animals that he has allowed to survive – the arrogance of a single species dictating the terms for what appears to be a natural history. The irony is that while some creatures are regarded as vermin they are also conserved for the chase. Hunted and harried for

Straw ricks were for centuries the traditional way that corn was stored with a thatched roof to shed the rain and keep the contents dry. Today only seen as historical farm exhibits but they once had an ecology all of their own

centuries the fox is well known for its cunning and crafty behaviour, which has no doubt helped it to survive. Indeed so well established is the sleek brown fox, even moving into towns, that despite persecution, its place as a predator down on the farm is as assured now as it was in the past. Yet why the badger should have been so maligned and mistreated by baiting with dogs through the centuries is difficult to understand. Even its very name means to torment or bait.

There are many former features of farmland which have slowly but surely gone. A time when horsepower was measured in hands and the rick was a seasonal structure, built to a traditional design. Cut grass laid to dry was carefully piled and combed, to shed the inevitable rain. Later in the year the harvest would have seen fields of cut corn, tied in sheafs and stacked six to the stook, row upon row of grain-laden straw drying beneath a blue September sky.

Within a few days farm-hands turned to the construction of the ricks. This was a skilled and painstaking rural art, the ricks thatched on top and round or rectangular in shape, according to the local custom and containing separate layers of barley, wheat or oats or perhaps just one variety. Often two or three ricks would be built not far from a threshing barn or in another sheltered spot on dry ground.

COUNTRY SEASONS

January

In the first month of the new year when the north or east wind blows the countryside can indeed be covered in snow. It's a time when mammal tracks, especially show up, as the greatest difficulty of watching wild animals is knowing where to look. The making of detailed notes and even a map will lead you back when the snow has gone.

February

Lengthening days bring hazel catkins and on warm wet nights the mass movements of frogs towards their spawning ponds. After dark the hooting calls of tawny owls mark out their territories and announce the beginning of their breeding season. On mild days the sound of woodpeckers drumming and song birds singing are a sign of spring towards the end of the month.

March

Mad March hares engaging in their boisterous, energetic chases compete for mates. Warm weather may rouse the hedgehog, thin after its winter sleep and eager to feed. Down in the copse the first spring flowers bring welcome colour – sweet violet, bright lesser celandine and later banks of primroses beneath the massed white blooms of the buckthorn blossom.

April

Young badgers and foxes appear above ground. Woodlands and valleys now wake to the rising dawn chorus, and the first swallows begin to arrive. Cowslips flower and more migrant birds fly in as the warmer weather sees bats become active and the common dormouse awake. The countryside is blooming beneath the still bare trees and the frenzy of nesting resident birds peak with the first fledglings.

May

Mayflowers burst and the dawn chorus begins earlier as the days continue to draw out. One of the last migrant birds to arrive is the swift which spreads with the summer to the north. The first butterflies to appear are those that over-winter, such as brimstone and small tortishells, while the orange tip emerges from pupation.

June

Apple trees draped in blossom and the constant hum of bees are the sights and sounds of the orchard. Yet within a few weeks the first petals begin to fall, and the activity of wild birds in spring gives way to the now subdued songs at dawn in the growing heat of the mid-summer sun. The first dragonflies emerge to flutter or hawk around the pond, and along the edge of a path by night tiny points of light appear as glow worms lure a mate.

July

In the early hours of darkness a female hedgehog may bring a snuffling band of young out on their first forage. Butterflies by day are now conspicuous especially out across the grassland, where hedge and meadow browns, blues and skippers fly. Down below amongst tangled stems the high pitched squeaks of shrews reveal their presence in tiny runs, and grasshoppers call from tall summer grass.

August

Mixed flocks of warblers and tits may be heard more than seen on a woodland walk beneath the dense canopy of broad-leafed trees. Most migrant birds and young will be feasting on the abundance of insect life in preparation for their long journey south. In fine weather a prolonged dry spell will bring many birds to the pond to drink, and some, such as the swallow, do not even land, quenching their thirst by surface skimming in flight.

September

Damp and wet in late summer this is the season for fungal growth, mushrooms in the meadows and a colourful variety of toadstools beneath the trees. Orchard windfalls are attracting hornets and wasps, butterflies and birds, all feasting on the rotting fruit. As the apple crop ripens the corn harvest has been gathered from the fields. With modern efficiency leaving little spilt grain, flocks of finches are attracted by the remaining arable weeds.

October

The fruits of autumn are providing a glut of food, as birds attack hedgerow berries and woodmice collect fallen hazel nuts. Dormice are agile enough to reach the thinnest branches and the surest way to discover the small mammals in a copse is to look at the shell remains – different creatures open nuts in entirely different ways.

November

More birds arrive to feed in the orchard, flocks of starlings, redwings and fieldfares. Days become noticeably shorter and increasing frosts force bats, hedgehogs and dormice into hibernation. Autumn gales may already have stripped the trees of leaves exposing the tangled twig nest of squirrels and the similar domed structure built by the magpie.

December

On clear, cold nights the sound of courting foxes will travel far especially the screech of a vixen. Mistletoe berries gleam white against bright green leaves and deep blue sky, a sticky food for thrushes. With the approach of the shortest day birds have less time to feed and longer nights to roost and so come eagerly to food put out around the house.

The fox is an adaptable predator of considerable success common today everywhere, from remote forests to farmland and suburban gardens. Active when people are not, at dawn, dusk and at night, the cubs stay close to home for the first few weeks after emerging

Rickyards once attracted their own community of wildlife. Apart from visiting crows and magpies and the occasional pheasant, all feeding on fallen grain spilt from the stack, strawricks supported several smaller birds. In harsh winter weather a surplus of grain was a vital supply of food for seed-eating flocks. A resident yellowhammer was often joined by others of its race during the colder months, feeding first over stubble fields and then around the ricks. Chaffinches too once gleaned their seed this way as did a less common sparrow. The tree sparrow lives away from farm buildings, out in the fields and along hedgerows. Like its house-living relative it is a gregarious bird, flocking in winter and breeding in loose little groups.

The ricks were seldom disturbed until the end of January when threshing could begin. Taken apart in stages they revealed and scattered more grain to the ever-increasing flocks of small birds. The destruction of these temporary straw buildings also disturbed other wild residents. Up to sixty tiny long-tailed rufous backed harvest mice have been counted running from a rick being demolished, showing clearly against the snow-scattered field as they made for another rick or nearby hedge. The house mouse could also be found in quantity, but only where the number of rats was low. Where ricks were being pulled apart and families of rats were leaping for their lives, few small mice would be found as rats will feed on their young.

41

The house mouse has long lived with people down through many ages. Thriving as much on the spillage of cultivated crops as in the shelter of man-made homes. Wherever people populated this mouse was never far behind unwittingly carried by man

Rodent-infested rickyards inevitably attract animals in search of a meal. Stoats and weasels sometimes hunted and even lived beneath the same straw roof as their prey, and farm cats would regularly visit as part of their daily and nocturnal rounds. The barn owl too included the ricks on its nightly hunt, its floating white form hovering and silently flapping round and round. Sitting on top, its buff-coloured back matched the shade of the straw, while it surveyed the scene with intense black eyes set in a heart-shaped face.

These picturesque and nostalgic structures have today been replaced by unsightly iron-clad coverings housing tightly bound bales of straw or hay. Over the decades this ugly though durable material has become an unlikely new home for wildlife. The popular use of corrugated tin roofing on sheds, barns and outbuildings is a modern feature which at least may rust in time. Damaged and forgotten, or windblown to some distant corner, discarded sheets give cover to the runs and nests of field voles and mice. Beneath a rusty tin roof they are relatively safe from aerial attack and most terrestrial predators, though the equally small weasel can steal under the ridges.

Warmed by the rays of a morning or afternoon sun the metal's radiant heat is attractive to cold-blooded creatures. Slow worms especially will bask in safety beneath its warm surface. In more shady places, on damp ground or partly covering a stream, the sheets can shelter frogs and toads, grass snakes or newts, or even fish in deep water.

From the first few natural glades deep in the wildwood, millions of acres of green pasture grew. Today there are more than one hundred and fifty different species of grass growing in wild Britain, yet the vast green covering which cloaks most of the farming land is more often a strain developed and sown by man.

Lacking the floral variety of old-fashioned leys, modern fields not only look quite different but apparently have a correspondingly dull taste. It was discovered during Ancient Farm trials that a mixture of wild grasses, grown with an abundance of flowers, produced a more tasty hay. Farm stock actually preferred the primitive fodder. When supplies eventually ran out it took them several days and increasing hunger to accept the modern day, botanically bland equivalent.

Since 1939 the average size of field has grown over fifty times and the nature of farms has radically changed. Grass is the vital ingredient providing the colour for the best part of this pleasant land, covering well over half the entire country. One year may see a temporary sward, the field sown, grazed or harvested before being ploughed in again – another year the same field may yield a yellow sea of oil-seed rape or an ocean of corn. It is a relentless

A random pattern of fields and hedgerows characterise Britain's traditional farmland. Where trees are retained, the richness of wildlife is enhanced as in large parts of this view over the South Hams of Devon

cycle which has seen the demise of many sights and sounds of the latter-day farm – the corncrakes' harsh grating cry once typified the call of mid-summer meadows both by day and even more by night. A shy and secretive seasonal visitor which once bred across the country, the corncake is confined today to traditional pastures and only Ireland and the Hebrides are favoured as summertime haunts, before it returns south to winter in Africa.

Arable farming is thought to have first begun on chalk downlands, where the thin soil could have been easily cultivated after felling a few trees. Within a few years and a similar number of crops the land reverted to grass and grazing was allowed. Generations of cattle and sheep feeding on the downs produced a fine cropped turf rich in wild flowers.

A marked decline in sheep during the nineteen thirties saw a corresponding rise in the rabbit population and woollen flocks were replaced as the principal grazer. Whether mown by rabbits or sheep, downland pasture retains its characteristic turf. Despite being relatively infertile as a soil, constant grazing favoured the growth of small, slow growing species. Grasses differ from other flowering plants as the leaves have their growing point at the base. Removal of the top growth does not therefore kill the overall growth. Indeed continual nibbling not only promotes the growth of grass and sedge but also flowers which grow close to the ground – plantains, stemless thistles, hawkweeds, hawkbits and salad burnet. In some parts orchids too can thrive, the common spotted being one of the earliest in June, followed by the pyramidal and the beautiful little bee orchid. Incredibly slow to reach full flowering height it may take the latter six to eight years to develop from tiny wind-blown seed to extraordinary bloom.

In 1953 plague swept through the rabbit world. In terms of population killed, myxomatosis was far more devastating than the human Black Death, and its consequences just as far-reaching. It almost wiped the rabbit out. With few sheep left to graze, the chalk downlands at first burst into colour as wild flowers grew as never before. Then within a few years coarse grasses and hawthorn shrubs began to appear, and the flowers slowly decreased. Only where mown by man or managed with new grazing flocks did the downs survive.

Another traditional pasture was the water meadow, a low-lying area flooded on purpose by the farmer. A complex series of channels and sluices ensured control of water levels. The meadows were only drowned for a few days in late winter – a technique which warmed the soil and prevented freezing. An added bonus was a fine rich layer of silt deposited on the surface. This produced an early flush of grass for lambs and ewes when other food was scarce or slow growing; the meadows were then left for hay. Sometimes

Opposite: Marsh orchids and ragged robin bloom with buttercups in an old wet meadow. As it may take several years for an orchid to grow from wind blown seed to flowering head the ground must remain undisturbed

they were even flooded during summer droughts but this limited the floral spread of primroses and cowslips, though it allowed the fritillary to flourish. A wealth of wild flowers once grew where today the tell-tale undulations of the ground are the only remaining marks of the one-time water meadow.

The loss of a permanent green sward with its growth of floral diversity is thought to be one of the main reasons for the decline in butterfly numbers. Many of these bright-winged warm-weather fliers feed in their larval stages on native grasses and flowers: the adonis blue on horseshoe vetch and silver spotted skipper on sheep's fescue; the meadow brown on meadow grass, common blue on birds-foot-trefoil and the small blue, the caterpillars of which feed on kidney vetch.

Changes in farming practice may at first be seen only as a saving in time or an increase in yield, but the effects can be catastrophic for some wild species. Grazed fields provide little cover for nesting birds, as most of the long grass goes early in the year. Fenced off from stock for hay, other fields were traditionally cut in July – ample time for birds and mammals, and a whole host of insects to rear their broods or emerge as fully fledged adults.

It is a trend which has spread to all parts of the countryside from fields to hedgerows, woods to wetlands. Even in the country time costs money, and with the speed of progress many species have been denied the time to adapt to the changing pace of life on the farm. It is time which has been taken from the meadows where late hay-making was the annual event. The modern farm would expect to cut the same field for silage at least twice – the first in early summer, the second within a few months.

Farm animals have come a long way since the days of auroch and wild boar. In Britain today the only big game to be seen on most farms are the herds of multi-coloured cattle, sheep, horses and pigs. These docile descendants whose wild ancestors coped with wolves, are fed and watered, housed and treated for injury or illness. Yet despite their cosetted surroundings cattle can still contribute to the natural life of the field.

Cowpats are the essential diet of dung beetles, and also attract many

DISAPPEARING DEER

The element of surprise is one of the principal appeals of watching wildlife, and yet a summer walk through a favourite wood may produce no more than a few of the expected birds and the tail end of a squirrel. Another time could bring you face to face with some rarely seen wild animal. But a quiet approach, walking into the wind with the sun at your back, is far better than spreading your scent before your imminent arrival.

From the edge of a forest clearing standing only a few paces away, an ear twitching deer had stepped into the streaming sunlight. Sensing it was not alone, but unsure of the danger, it too froze in its stride. After a few seconds that seemed more like minutes the roe deer left with a leap.

The way that mammals can apparently melt into cover was shown by a herd of sika deer. Disturbed by a party of people they vanished into the rampant rhododendron bush. The male apparently unhindered by the size of his multi-pointed antlers. It was only when attempting to follow their tracks that the impossible had seemingly been done. Their escape was made through a tangled roof tunnel barely wide enough for a person let alone a stag.

An otter leaves a gentle rippled wake as it paddles quietly upstream. A rare and endangered mammal in modern times, they have suffered through the pollution of rivers and an intolerance of regular disturbance

different flies. On warm humid days clouds of flying insects pester the stock, and attract the field-skimming swallows which feast on the swarms. At dusk and after dark the hunt for insect life is taken up in the air by bats, while badgers dig in the dung for beetles and worms. With the coming of dawn and dew-soaked grass, flocks of starlings fly into the fields. Feeding at the feet of cattle whose giant hooves flush out grasshoppers and flies, the birds fan out alongside their bovine beaters.

The very basis of farming is the fertility of the land – good growth and healthy stock are dependant upon the quality of the soil. As the natural cover of much of the country was once the floor of the deciduous forest, the native fauna and flora of the soil is essentially that of the wood.

A remarkable mixture of minerals from those in rocks to those released by the dead and dying, is inextricably bound to the cycle of earthly life, which encompasses single-celled to burrowing mammals, bacteria to higher plants, is the life which creates and is the soil. The richer the medium the more

Overleaf: Corn sheaves left six to a stook are arranged in rows north to south for drying, the final stage of the traditional harvest prior to being carted away and stored in a rick before threshing

living organisms there are and one of the wealthiest is that of the deciduous wood. Of all the creatures that dwell below ground the earthworm is one of the most important. Pulling fallen leaves down into their burrows, worms consume the surface litter and begin the conversion to humus. Insects and mites help to fragment plant matter and fungi and bacteria break down the material still further.

Nutrients released are then recycled and taken up by living plants. But the bulk of what is left is known as humus: black and lacking structure it coats the surface particles, and adds to the stable and structural nature of the soil. This web of lowly life forms the base of the nutritional tree and is an important reservoir of food even for animals much further up the nutritional scale.

Comparatively large predators such as badgers and foxes will consume huge quantities of earthworms at times. The flocks of gulls which gather at ploughing time are a typical sight in certain parts of the country. Even buzzards have been known to follow in the wake of the tractor – but not just for worms, a whole series of mice and even moles are turned up by the progress of the plough.

The power of modern machinery would have been unimaginable to farmers just a few generations ago, of size and speed almost beyond belief. Where once a man and two shires trod and cut a single furrow, the roar of over two hundred horsepower carves a broad swathe with up to seven steel shares – all in a day's work. As the world of the top soil turns a mass of wriggling and writhing life is briefly exposed on the surface. Frantic flocks of rooks, lapwings, jackdaws and blackheaded gulls feast on the upturned offering, landing almost before the soil has settled behind the plough.

At summer's end, fields of ripened corn await the arrival of the latest reaper. Massive, gaudily coloured combine harvesters sail with terrifying sound across the sea of corn. Waves of straw lie in lines down the field, left in the wake of the combine's noise and accompanying clouds of gently swirling dust. Far more grain appears to be spilt by today's machines than ever before, but modern practice denies wildlife this food source because of the

Haymaking on a traditional farm sees the dried grass baled and stored in the barn. Centuries-old ways established a seasonal pattern exploited by many different wild mammals and birds built a wildlife dependent for its future on continued farming practise

speed of subsequent operations. On some farms most of the remaining straw is baled and removed while on others large quantities are burned on the field, before being ploughed into the ground. Even just a few days grace, however, would see an increase in natural life, as nature's gleaners reap the benefits of the delay. The increase in field voles and mice is eagerly taken by twilight hunting barn owls, as the end of summer is the time when their young are newly fledged.

Traditionally the centre of farming life is a complex of buildings, the yard and farmhouse, these often surrounded by shrubs, wonderfully wild gardens and an orchard of lichen encrusted trees. These features add to its rural appeal not just for man but for wildlife as well, and create an oasis on a well kept farm. Even birds and insects are encouraged where not welcome out on the rest of the farm. Some species have changed with the times and adapted to new conditions. The swallow was once well known to nest inside the large chimneys of country kitchens. Changes in culinary habits and the advent of compact cookers saw a trend towards smaller chimneys, and the chimney-dwelling swallows became a nester in barns – another man-made substitute for a cave. Along with jackdaws, starlings and sparrows, the house martin, swift and swallow have all taken with some success to farm buildings.

51

High banked hedgerows flanking a lane lead down to a farm house beyond. Primroses left unpicked are today one of the benefits brought about by the increasing awareness of nature left in its place, rather than picked and taken away

Many of these birds and the various rodents have at one time or another all fallen prey to a feline hunter. The farm cat, tabby or ginger, black, white or both, has and will no doubt continue to be a major predator around farms. For at least fifteen hundred years domestic and feral cats have been stalking the wildlife of the country. But unlike natural predators which breed only once a year, the domesticated cat gone wild can retain its remarkable reproductive rate. While rabbits are renowned for their prodigious progeny the cat can be almost as prolific. Even when fed and pampered by man they remain innate killers, taking a heavy toll in the spring of fledgling birds, as well as the rodents they are supposed to reduce.

The countryside today is as much a natural legacy as a reminder of our own history on the land, indeed even the word for field owes its origin to the Old English "feld" – an area felled from the forest. Despite the many changes and ravages of time, traditional farmland often retains many of its ancestral traits – plants and animals from a prehistoric age and structures from beyond living memory. Take a walk through any deciduous wood and you can see that legacy still standing to the present day. From giant oak to the smallest shrub a past age of trees has given way to one of the surrounding farm – a mere sixty human lives, yet just six for the oak.

3 THE OLD BARN

Standing in the corner of a field the walls of a forgotten building are gently crumbling with time. Rotting timbers support a roof of rusted iron, now bending with the weight of years of neglect. The old barn is today seemingly no more than a monument to a bygone age. Yet over the centuries, and even in its heyday, it sheltered not only the farm's stock and winter feed but wildlife and wild stories as well. In the twilight of the day's end the glimpse of a silently flying white apparition and the sound of an eerie screaming cry from the shadows of a deserted barn, have given rise to many a ghostly tale. The reality is a bird so familiar to farmers and countrymen in the past, that it was named after one of its favourite haunts. The barn owl is the most spectacular and best known of all the denizens of farm buildings.

The structure of barns was born of practical necessity, fulfilling a function of farm life, rather than any benevolence towards wildlife. But many old barns feature an owl window, built into an end wall beneath the gabled eaves, providing not only ventilation for the hayloft but access for owls. As a catcher of rodents the barn owl was considered a friend of the farmer and as such was to be encouraged.

Barns were often built away from the busy life of the farmyard and so remained undisturbed for much of the year. They are today just as important for the survival of the barn owl as they were in the past for encouraging the spread of the species. It was more by accident than design that the construction of barns in the past created ideal places for barn owls to rest and breed; nesting in dark seclusion either on top of massive cob and stone walls or down amongst old bales of hay. Even places to roost away from the nest were provided. To the workman who made the barn they were beams to support the roof; for the owl a safe place to perch. The barn, however, is far more than just a daytime retreat or a nest site for owls. During hard winter weather a hay-filled barn can provide an insulated shelter in a snowladen landscape. But perhaps even more important than warmth, barns can also provide food for a snowbound owl. Whether in search of a meal, or somewhere to nest, rodents are also attracted to barns. And when bad weather prevents an owl flying outside it can survive by hunting indoors. Yet only a few days of continuous deep snow can cause an owl to die of starvation. This is perhaps one of the main factors which confines the barn owl to mainly low-lying countryside. Heavy rain, too, will prevent an owl hunting but for different reasons to snow. The soft, loose plumage of the barn

An old barn far from the nearest beaten track holds a secret shared only by the farmer's family. A pair of barn owls have nested up on the hay loft floor, 'from a time where memory is not' as the old country saying quotes

owl is easily soaked and rain hampers hearing and vision. Snow not only hides any prey but restricts the activity of mice and voles to underground tunnels and stored food. Perhaps, surprisingly, cold weather alone may actually assist the owl in the search for prey. On a clear cold night the rustlings of small mammals on frost-covered ground is more easily heard.

At the end of a warm spring day, as shadows draw across the fields, the sky turns shades of crimson above a setting sun. A barn owl emerges from its daytime roost, ready to begin the hunt. With senses almost beyond our belief, barn owls can see in almost total dark and pinpoint the slightest sound. Their eyes are perhaps a hundred times more sensitive than our own and, even on the darkest of cloudy nights, there is still enough light for them to see their prey – conditions in which we are helplessly blind. Large forward-looking eyes surrounded by a feathery facial disc which also hides enormous ear openings, are a feature of owls. For, no less remarkable than their eyesight, the hearing of barn owls is just as extraordinary. Concealed by feathers and acting as huge sound-gathering funnels, the owls' hidden ears enable them to focus on the rustling movement of prey. Field voles, shrews, rats and mice are the main quarry of the barn owl, but small birds and even bats, as well as insects, will occasionally be taken.

In flight the barn owl is almost silent. Soft downy plumage covers its body, from hooked beak to daggerlike claws. Raised barbs along the feathers of the wing's leading edge reduce noise still further. The slow, graceful yet purposeful beat of barn owl wings, as the bird floats across a meadow, belies the constantly scanning senses. Detecting a vole, the owl suddenly dives, sometimes throwing itself sideways, dropping straight down or even performing a partial somersault, head first with wings held wide. Only at the last moment does it lift its head and swing the feet down to where its head was only a split second before. Talons open and the prey is caught and killed. For a few moments the bird remains on the ground, wings spread across the grass, before lifting off almost as suddenly and silently as it arrived. A long low glide across the valley and the owl returns to the barn, pausing briefly on a farm gate to transfer its catch from claws to beak, leaving its feet clear to land.

The sheer efficiency of an owl's hunting ability can be quite awesome. At times it may return to its mate or young every few minutes, carrying yet another mouse or vole. Owls are creatures of habit, hunting the same ground over and over again, in exactly the same way. Regular beats may be visited several times in the same night. Their light almost buoyant flight quickly quartering the ground, generally follows the edge of a woodland or field,

Roosting high in the barn roof an owl can safely survey the scene and make good an escape if disturbed. From dawn to dusk this may be its regular secluded retreat, away from the bright sunlight

ITCHES AND OWLS

The barn owl is one of the most spectacular and elusive birds of traditional farming country; not only nocturnal and shy but tending to breed in some of the most remote and lonely old buildings. Being rare and endangered they are protected by law and so any observation or photography done at or near its nest must only be done after obtaining a Nature Conservancy licence.

At many locations vehicular access is difficult and to avoid any undue disturbance a quiet approach must be made on foot. The construction of a hide the previous winter, while the owls were away from the barn, gave a hidden view of the normal nest site. Up beneath the rafters where old dust covered cobwebs still hung, a wooden structure had been built on and surrounded by bales of hay.

As parents returned to feed their young it was compulsive viewing with only one slight irritation and that was the fleas. The barn was also sometimes used by poultry from the not too distant farm and unfortunately some of their parasites still remained to pester any intruder. The only consolation was that having tasted their mistake they left, leaving me literally itching to see the owls.

often below hedge height, alternately flapping and gliding, sometimes in a deliberate line, at others twisting and turning, even back-tracking and hovering briefly on outstretched heraldic wings. When food is easily obtained they may also hunt in a less energetic fashion, flying from post to post along a fence, using gates or any convenient perch and watching intently for any movement or sound – a tactic that is more akin to the tawny owl.

In common with all birds of prey and many others, the barn owl produces a pellet of indigestible remains, several hours after a meal. Instead of being excreted, along with other waste matter, it is regurgitated through the mouth as a compact mass of fur, feathers and bones. Over the years large quantities of pellets may build up on the barn floor below and around the nest site. They are valuable indicators, not just of a barn owl's presence and regular use of a building, but, when analysed, of the day-to-day diet of an owl. A calling card left wherever an owl stays, the pellet enables an overall picture of its prey to be built.

Eventually the pellets dry out and, from their initial shiny black, turn to a powdery grey. Slowly breaking up they add to the debris of the barn, but not before a tiny moth has lived out its life cycle. More commonly known as the curse of the wardrobe, the clothes' moth perhaps originally lived in bird pellets, long before mankind took to wearing skins and animal fur. Their caterpillars, and those of a few other species, consume the softer parts that the owl's digestion could not reach. In a shaft of sunlight cutting through the dust-filled air of an old hayloft, a swarm of miniature moths rises at the slightest touch. The air teems with tiny glistening wings for just a few moments before the moths settle down and scuttle for cover.

A traditional nesting barn will also be the focal point of the barn owl's

Opposite: The barn owl will hunt night and sometimes day for its principal prey of field voles. Returning to feed her brood the prey is transferred from foot to beak before entering the barn, either in flight or after alighting on a nearby branch or roof

When winter snow prevents a barn owl from hunting they can only sit and wait for the thaw that will once more uncover their prey. But always remaining alert as the occasional mouse can appear in or around the barn

territory, usually held by the male. But while some owls remain paired throughout the year, roosting close to each other, indulging in mutual preening and making surprisingly conversational sounds of squeaking and chirruping, other pairs maintain a more casual association. They remain in the same territory yet roost in separate barns and their only contact is an occasional visit to each other or a chance meeting during nocturnal excursions.

Whatever the relationship, the owls' return to the nesting barn in March marks the beginning of breeding for the year. Throughout the month and into April, the male's territorial screech can be heard echoing around the barn. Each evening he leaves at about the same time to hunt the surrounding meadows, returning to present food to his mate. A plentiful supply soon brings her into breeding condition. It is now that a curious behavioural change takes place, akin to that sometimes seen in courting humans. The female reverts to juvenile ways, making the strange snoring hiss which is so characteristic of these birds. Standing around just like a youngster, she awaits the male's return, to be fed.

Mating and mutual preening are very much part of the barn owls' private life at this time of the year. Sitting close to each other the male is seen to be much smaller than his mate. Rubbing cheeks, clicking their tongues and fencing with bills is a prelude to the main event of the season. Barn owls make no attempt to build a nest. The male simply chooses a suitable site, and the female then lays her eggs amongst the soft debris of pellets lying on the hay. Five white eggs are usually laid, one every two or three days. They soon lose their initial whiteness as they become soiled in the rather messy conditions of the nest.

Even by day the depths of a barn are sparsely lit. In a darkened corner the dim figure of an owl sits quietly on her eggs, eyes closed; the vigil has begun. The muted sounds of the countryside drift in on the wind – an occasional sheep or cow, a tractor or passing crow.

Just before the eggs begin to hatch the female can be heard uttering a soft twittering call in response to the call from a chick, still held within its shell. After about thirty days the first of the brood begins to hatch. A tiny hole in the egg is made by a hard scale on the tip of the chick's beak; known as an egg tooth it is a means of escape and will later be shed. The birth of a baby barn owl often starts in the evening. By the early hours of the following morning the stillness of the barn is broken by an ungainly little chick struggling into the world. Pot-bellied, pink-skinned and covered only in sparse white down still wet from the hatch, it is almost helpless and very vulnerable at first.

The eggs hatch as they were laid and so there can be as much as two weeks between the eldest and youngest of the brood. Sometimes not all the eggs hatch and even if they do, not all the young survive. The oldest and strongest chick will take the first available food. In a bad year, when rodent prey is scarce or hunting difficult because of the weather, only one or two chicks will eventually fledge from the nest.

Female barn owls tend to sit very tight when disturbed. Many a farmer moving bales in a barn has been surprised by an owl leaving her nest at the very last second, no doubt saving many eggs and young from unintentional destruction. Continued disturbance, though, will force a desertion, especially from newly laid eggs. Any eggs which do not hatch soon disappear, trampled into the steadily growing layer of pellets. The maternal instinct of barn owls is usually well developed. One female was even seen assisting a chick to hatch from its egg, breaking off bits of membrane and shell, then cleaning the young chick of embryonic remains – a rare sight in the bird world. The day after hatching an owlet is already strong enough to be able to utter its begging call, a series of hissing and chittering sounds. When all the young have hatched, the raucous reception for an adult returning with food has to be heard to be believed.

For ten days or more the female remains on the nest brooding the young closely, especially in cold weather and as protection from possible predators. While eggs are known to have been taken by jackdaws and ravens, owlets are less likely to be threatened as long as the female remains close by. But it is not unknown for a stoat to be found high in the hayloft of a barn. They are remarkably agile and surprisingly good at climbing walls and trees. In one

THE CROSSING OF PATHS

The warmth of an early summer day was beginning to fade with the approach of evening light, and just below the ridge of a hill the long meadow grass grew still as the breeze died away. Across the valley a miniature black and white stream of dairy cows poured out of a distant farm and made their way back into the fields. On predictable paths their progress is a regular event timed by the farmers watch.

Less predictable but still at times incredibly precise are the movements of many wild mammals and birds. Keeping to a set pattern may appear to hold inherent dangers yet the survival value of well known paths seems to outweigh the risks. Just as the field vole has a pattern of runs so the barn owl will hunt the same haunts. But add to that the unpredictable movements of people and the ever changing elements, combined with the seasonal abundance of food, then a planned watching of wild-life becomes more of a chance encounter.

The words of wisdom and greeting in Britain seldom change with the season; 'But the weather is never usually as bad as this,' or, 'You should have been here yesterday, it was a wonderful sight, shame they have all gone'. Bearing that in mind, a farmers prediction of a barn owl's exact path and time of appearance was listened to with a degree of disbelief. 'He usually appears over the top of that gate at quarter past eight, then turns and flies alongside the hedge, up the far side of the field across into the next and down the other side.'

Getting into position and setting up the camera well ahead of schedule can often mean a wait of many hours or every-thing happening within minutes. When eventually the silent white wings of a barn owl rose beyond the old farm gate and swept down to hunt in floating flight across the meadow, lit by the dying rays of a red-balled sun, no-one was more surprised than me to learn that the time was eight sixteen.

Only a day-and-a-half old, a barn owl chick bears little resemblance to the adult. The first to hatch with two eggs still left, its nest-mate at less than an hour old has yet to gain the strength to lift its head for more than a few seconds

barn where owls were found not to be breeding for the first time in many years, a cause for the desertion was sought as no other suitable nest sites were in the area. A harmless tunnel trap set up in the loft soon caught the culprit – a stoat. Two months later a pair of barn owls began breeding again and, rather later than usual, managed to raise a fine brood of three.

At first owlets are fed on scraps torn off by the parents, but soon begin to swallow small mice and shrews whole. They seldom take food from the floor, waiting for a parent to dangle it overhead. Tiny bristles at the base of the beak are touched by offered prey which then stimulates the youngster to eat. When the youngest owlet is about ten days old the female begins to leave the nest for lengthening periods. She assists her mate with the hunt to satisfy the growing demands of the chicks. The owlets' eyes open for the first time after two weeks, by which time a second dense covering of down is already beginning to grow. At this age the young are remarkably gawky-looking creatures, and in complete contrast to the beauty of the adult, can only be described as positively ugly. Their looks, however, are outweighed by their comical nature, which develops over the weeks as their plumage begins to grow. They twist their heads until almost upsidedown, bobbing and peering intently at any strange sound. With the growth of more feathers and a facial disc they soon assume the familiar features of the owl.

The brown rat was also unintentionally spread by man, and as a carrier of disease and despoiler of stored grain it is definitely no friend of the farmer

There is one extraordinary feature of young barn owl behaviour that seems contrary to some other birds of prey. The occasional disappearance of the youngest bird from a nest is well known, and cannibalism is suspected; but unlike the golden eagle, where the eldest will kill and often eat the youngest, this appears not to be the norm for British barn owls. What has been observed is an older member of a brood actually feeding a younger, behaviour unknown in any other bird. Yet despite parental and apparently even unique sibling care the average brood is seldom more than four.

Barn owls first leave the nest at around sixty days when wing flapping exercise gives way to first faltering flight. They are extremely playful at this age as they develop the skills necessary to hunt and capture prey. A setting sun and lengthening shadows around the old ruined barn herald the evening's activity. Young owls pouncing on pellets, leaves, sticks and stones, follow one another from beam to bale and back again, exploring anything and everything they can, accompanied by an excited chorus of snoring and chirruping calls. If a parent suddenly arrives with food, a mad dash and flurry

Opposite: Preening is an important part of a bird's daily routine, especially for owls as their soft downy feathers evolved for silent flight easily become soiled and waterlogged, and that may impair its hunting ability limiting its chances of survival

of wings ensue as all return to the nest, demanding to be fed.

At first the newly independent owlets remain around the barn, while the parents continue to return with food. They learn the techniques of hunting by chasing moths, beetles and even slow-moving craneflies. They spend much of their time on the ground, running in their strange ungainly way after anything which moves, but their chances of catching small mammals are hampered by their incessant calls – sounds which probably alert any potential prey well in advance.

From egg to adult, barn owls take an extraordinary three months or more to mature. Dependence on their parents is gradually reduced as the adults return less often with food, and then finally ceases. Remaining for a while in the vicinity of the home barn, the young may still chase a parent for food. Wanderings take them further into the surrounding countryside and as the days pass the young owls' confidence grows with experience. By now they are roosting on their own in nearby buildings or conifers or holly trees – wherever there is good cover during the hours of light. Eventually they may be driven from the parents' territory, usually by the female, as the days become shorter in late summer or if food becomes scarce. As voles are their principal prey, any annual fluctuation in vole numbers is reflected in the success or failure of barn owl breeding. Even in a good year when prey is easily found, many other factors limit the owls' chances of survival.

Barn owls are perhaps the most widespread land bird in the world, and are found on almost every continent. In the more northerly parts of their range, hard winters take a heavy toll of first year birds. In northern Europe less than one in ten will survive to see the spring, most dying of starvation during the coldest months of the year.

Even from the beginning of an owl's independence its first flights are not without danger. If it lands in wet grass, its soft feathers quickly become waterlogged and, unable to take off again, the owl is likely to be killed by a predator or by exposure. When drawn to water to drink or bathe, a steepsided cattle trough can become a death trap for the birds. It is possible that a young inexperienced owl, seeing its mirrored image in still water for the first time, attacks the reflection with tragic consequences. Away from the barn, some birds are attracted by rich pickings along the wide grassy verges of motorways. Sadly many an owl's fate has been sealed when swept into the slipstream of passing traffic. Combined with the hazards of collision with overhead wires, trains or large windows of country houses, the accidental mortality of young owls in their first few months is high. Add to that the risk of being shot or poisoned by the irresponsible and ill-informed it is surprising that any survive at all.

Yet, provided with suitable hunting grounds and undisturbed nesting sites,

Opposite: A kestrel's eye view from within a barn reveals a fledgling tactic for keeping its newly arrived meal. While struggling to swallow the food it turns its back on the others and spreads its wings wide (*Photo: Roger Hosking*)

Set apart from the rest of the farm buildings and once nestled in the corner of a field, the old cob-walled barn stands alone in rural splendour, with rotting elms nearby, seldom visited by man from one year to the next

barn owls can maintain a remarkable breeding success. Certainly the rearing of two broods a year, while not common in recent times, was not unknown in the past. There are still a few barns where owls have nested and reared young annually well beyond the living memory of the farm. Yet perhaps even more incredible is, that while barn owls can live up to twenty years in captivity, the most recent record of the oldest wild owl in Britain was only eight years. The average age may even be less than two years.

Standing in the rural splendour of its own isolation the old barn can attract birds other than barn owls. The most common bird of prey is the kestrel, sometimes found nesting in surprisingly close proximity to owls. Strangely the birds appear to ignore each other when inside the barn. But outside it is the kestrel that will harass an owl caught in the open. Little owls too will nest in similar situations and in one barn all three birds reared their respective broods in the same season, just a few metres from each other. But taking the prize for being an unwelcome neighbour the noisy, often gregarious jackdaw is more of a risk to the owls since it steals not only the eggs but chicks as well. Jackdaws will build their untidy pile of sticks lined with wool in any convenient hole. What the jackdaw lacks in size, being one of the smallest of the crow family, it makes up for by its noisy garrulous gatherings outside the breeding season.

Kestrels and barn owls will not only nest in the same barn but feed on a surprisingly similar diet, though competition is reduced by behaviour – one hunting by day the other mainly at night. Most of the kestrels' hunting activity is concentrated at dawn and dusk, though the sight of a hovering kestrel is not unusual at any time of the day. Incredibly this distinction between day and night hunting is not as clear as it first seems. Kestrels have been seen to hunt at night aided by the light of a full moon, while barn owls are known to hunt during the day. Kestrels are adaptable birds, taking advantage of man's activities by following the plough, dropping into furrows in pursuit of small mammals. It is thought they may also take a large number of earthworms but smaller young birds, especially starlings and lapwings, are favoured prey. Kestrels, too, make no attempt to build a nest, usually choosing a soft ledge or taking over an old nest of another bird. At one site an attempt was made to use an owls' nest, but the kestrels were soon evicted when the original owners returned.

The female kestrel lays her eggs at two day intervals, not unlike the barn owl. So a clutch of five eggs, the usual size, may take nine days or more to complete. Kestrels nest from mid-April to May, and as incubation takes twenty-eight days they often hatch, at best, only a few weeks before the barn owl. This similarity between a falcon and an owl does not end just with their

This cave-dwelling bird changed the habits of a lifetime to live closer to man, first being renamed the chimney swallow before moving into barns. Garages and porchways are also used by these versatile and swift flying birds

HAUNT OF THE OWL

The first sight of a barn owl flying across a long shadowed meadow can leave an indelible memory, but one unfortunate owl left more than that behind. Not so much a lasting impression as the dusty imprint of wings and body on a window. Large expanses of glass claim many bird victims in mid-flight and those that survive are lucky only to have been stunned. The barn owl's soft downy feathers that aid its silent approach also produce quantities of white particles, that are generally shaken out with hay dust from the barns it frequents. The impact of the bird hitting that glass left the lines of its feathers as a ghostly impression of its passing.

Flying spectres glowing in the dark are occasionally reported and lead to many a spine chilling tale. But the most reasonable explanation for such ghost owls is not so boring as intriguing. Barn owls must sometimes roost in hollow rotten trees where luminous bacteria or honey fungus grow, a common source of apparently luminous wood. Covered in the dusty debris and fine particles of living fungal filaments the owl appears to glow an eerie phosphorescent sheen.

nest and prey — the female kestrel alone incubates the eggs, the male providing her with food. But the similarity ends with the time the young spend at the nest. After hatching, young kestrels mature much faster than owls and leave within the month. Incubation does not always begin with the first egg and so kestrel chicks are similar in size and leave the nest about the same time. Dispersing from the parental territory, some British kestrels tend to migrate towards the south and east. Crossing the Channel they will winter in southern Europe, seldom going further than the South of France. Surviving the winter they retrace that first flight and frequently return to the same area where they were born. Some kestrels do remain in Britain throughout the year and their numbers are increased, in eastern and central parts, by winter visitors from northern France, Holland and Scandinavia. These winter migrants return to their native countries in early spring.

In complete contrast to the rather random travels of individual kestrels, the far from lonely long-distance swallow migrates in large numbers. Collecting on overhead wires in late summer, before flying south for the winter, swallows are a familiar sight. Returning from South Africa in spring, flying after insects, they feed almost exclusively on the wing. Swallows are often found near horses and cattle, places where insects thrive. So it is natural enough that when it comes to breeding, swallows choose the nearest available overhead shelter. Beneath the hayloft and attached to one of the rafters is the swallow's nest. The birds use pellets of mud, from a nearby puddle or pond, mixed with saliva; grass, straw or hair, often picked up while in flight and mixed with the mud, bind the nest together. An old nail or small ledge provides all the support needed to begin the building. Both swallows share the construction process and the nest hardens rapidly in warm dry weather. Indeed, so strongly built are these cup-shaped nests that many may survive from year to year. Simple repairs and a new lining of feathers are

Opposite: Enormous ears sets the long-eared bat apart from all others except for the closely related grey form. During the day, in its summer roost barn, they keep to tiny crevices but if the roof becomes too warm they emerge to cool down on the rafters (*Photo: Roger Hosking*)

often the only addition each season. Most swallows manage to produce two broods of four or five young; in a good year sometimes three broods are reared.

The stock dove is another barn-dwelling bird during the breeding season and it, too, will sometimes raise three separate broods. Smaller than the closely related wood pigeon, stock doves sometimes build their nests in small colonies. In common with other doves and pigeons they rear their young on a regurgitated vegetable soup known as pigeon's milk. They are adaptable and yet inconspicuous birds seldom rearing more than two young at a time.

But while birds are the most obvious of the life that inhabits the barn, other creatures depend on this structure to survive. Of the fifteen different types of bat found in Britain only a few habitually frequent barns, either as a place for winter hibernation or, more often, as a summer roost and nursery for their young. The obvious risk to bats living near barns is borne out by the frequency of their remains found in barn owl pellets. It is no coincidence that natterers, long-eared, pipistrelle and noctule bats are those usually taken. All four are common and widespread across the country and all can be found in barns. Even one of our rarest bats, the greater horseshoe, will spend the summer months in a favoured barn, sometimes in large colonies. Kestrels, too, will take a surprising number of bats but it seems that while certain individuals like to eat these mammals, hunting them late into the evening, other kestrels seemingly ignore this aerobatic prey, preferring mice or voles.

For hibernation many bats will seek out either a cave or a stone building – places where severe fluctuations in the outside temperature are less likely to be felt. Sometimes bats shelter behind wooden boards and even in small spaces between wood joins, gaining access to a closed barn through the tiny gaps between roof slates. Holes in walls are also used, where mortar has weathered away, often providing a small entrance to a large cavity inside.

Farm buildings are especially important for bats during the summer months when the females leave their young literally hanging around in the barn. Such a collection of young bats is known as a nursery and may be left

THREATENING TO SURVIVE

Barn owls will react to danger or disturbance in many different ways. Some will simply fly out of a barn when someone enters, slipping through an exit in the opposite side without being seen. Others may sit tight or just hide. To watch an owl's response to sudden human intrusion is to see an instinctive reaction born of successful strategy. Perched on one leg an owl was asleep on a beam, but at the first sign of danger as a farmhand came in to collect a bale, the owl lowered its other leg, drew in its wings and stood tall. Eyes at first wide open narrowed to tiny slits and its buff-coloured wings were pulled across to hide its bright white chest. Although in full view the owl was neither seen nor disturbed and when the intruder had gone the bird relaxed once more.

Even young owls develop a spectacular threat and aggressive display which may one day be put to good use, should it ever be cornered. Wings open wide, tail feathers spread and raised, the head is lowered. Then with glaring eyes the owl puffs, hisses and makes an alarming beak clicking noise which is actually made by its tongue.

Supported on granite hewn pillars the open fronted hayloft of these old barns today lie forgotten but not unused. Both barn owl and kestrel as well as little owl have all bred beneath its tin roof in the past

alone while the adults are in search of food. It has been suggested that a single pipistrelle bat may, in one night, consume as many as 3,500 insects, many of which are probably considered as pests by both farmers and gardeners. As might be expected of a flying mammal that is both social and intelligent, the problem of finding its single young in the midst of the nursery has been overcome. From birth a strong bond exists between mother and baby and she is able to recognise its call from all the others. Even giving birth, in an upsidedown world where all stand on their heads, requires a special technique. The newborn bat is caught in a fold of its mother's tailskin. Gaining strength it then slowly climbs to the suckling position, clinging to its mother's fur. For the following few days the baby maintains its tight embrace, even when the mother flies. As the baby bat grows, gaining size and weight, the mother leaves it in the squeaking mass of fur and tiny membranous wings that is the summer nursery. At first the young bat spends much of the day close to its mother suckling frequently. By three weeks it begins to fly and just two weeks later, weaned and deserted, it can fend for itself.

For such small creatures bats are remarkably long lived – some reaching thirty years of age. But this life span is reflected in their breeding as they can be four or five years old before producing young. Some individuals are perhaps even nine or ten years old before they mature to full breeding

71

FACE OF A HUNTER

The facial disc of the barn owl is perhaps its most fascinating feature and one that it shares in common with other owls. It is no decorative adornment but a mask that hides the architecture of its head and holds the key to the effectiveness of its hunting precision. Above and below its eyes densely packed curving feathers form a wave collecting wall leading to a funnel that channels and concentrates the slightest of sounds. Overlain by a thin filmy layer of soft plumes a downy veil covers the face and effectively hides the huge tunnels that lead back to its ears. Even these openings are not symetrically placed and enable the owl to judge distance and direction more accurately when too dark to see. The information received by faint rustling sounds give far more to the face than meets the eyes, and last second mid-course corrections enable the owl to precisely predict the path of its prey.

The appearance of the face also alters with the alertness of the owl. When asleep the barn owl's peculiar heart shaped face is most clearly seen as the feathers are all laid back. Alert the disc becomes rounder and the direction finding facility enhanced.

condition. Each species of bat has its own preferred roost, and different places may be used each year with amazing regularity. The same long-eared bat may be found hibernating in a cave in December, roosting in a hollow tree in March and then breeding in a barn in June.

This seasonal use of a structure built by man is not just confined to bats. Certain butterflies overwinter in the same barn year after year. What is even more remarkable is that it is never the same butterfly, but a different generation and yet it can be found in exactly the same place. The small tortoiseshell and peacock are familiar garden butterflies abundant in late summer. By autumn the return of shorter days and colder nights sees the butterflies back at the barn. Entering through an open door, window or crack in the wall, they rest high above the floor. The cryptic brown coloration on the underside of their wings matches the timbers, darkened with age. Generally keeping well clear of dusty beams, draped with the cobwebs of years, butterflies seek out the cleaner corners of the barn. In the spring, and once more warmed into life, peacocks and small tortoiseshells fly away to produce a new generation. Occasionally a red admiral or comma butterfly will also spend the winter here, but the only signs of their stay are those left behind – tattered fragile wings hanging from the roof, the remains of a spider's meal.

The wind now gently whistles through a yawning gap in the rusted iron roof of a once-thatched barn. From the open-fronted loft, old hay hangs blowing in the breeze. A rotting ladder rests against weathered woodwork and the tools of the farmer's past trade still lie in scattered abandonment after many years. There is a nostalgic sadness about these decaying relics of another era. Yet as a refuge for wildlife their value cannot be denied. Were it not for the thousands of undisturbed old barns that are such a feature of farming country, barn owls and many other creatures might have gone the way of shire horses and hayricks.

4 FRUITS OF THE ORCHARD

A vast scattered fruit-bearing forest once covered much of lowland Britain – from Kent to Cornwall, west and east of Evesham to Hereford and north beyond the Humber. The charm that is England's green and pleasant land is set amongst the blossoms of the orchard. A planted parkland which typifies our country image abroad. The tranquil beauty of spring blossom, lush green grass and gleaming white-fleeced sheep grazing between the trees. Pears, plums and cherries feature in many parts of the country but the orchard which once grew alongside almost every farmhouse in the land, was the apple. A fruit which provided both food and liquor was a valued asset for any farm.

Today more than four thousand different varieties of apples are known, all of which owe their origin to the humble crab apple. Small and tart to the taste, the wild apple can still be found scattered throughout Eurasia. But the modern rich and succulent fruit from that wild stock is a product of man's patience – the crossing and recrossing of various strains for more than two thousand years. Although the first eating apples were originally introduced by the Romans, the cider orchard was a later legacy of the Normans. So, for nearly a thousand years, apple orchards have been a real part of the picture of farm life, a comparatively new place for nature to explore and exploit.

An orchard which, though often planted close to hand, yet is far enough away to be undisturbed for much of the year, is surprisingly rich in wildlife. And the creatures which now plunder the fruits of the farmer's past labour, do so mainly unseen.

Amongst a pastoral scene of hedgerows and cultivated fields the orchard's arboreal monoculture can be a wooded island in an agricultural sea. It does not, however, lay claim to a wildlife all of its own. Many birds spend only part of their year there, either feasting on fallen fruit in winter or nesting during spring and summer. But despite the young age of the orchard in Britain, its wild ancestor has an ancient history reflected in the ninety different species of insect known to be associated with the apple.

Lit by the low light of a winter's sun and lying no more than a stone's throw from the farmhouse, the gnarled and twisted trees of an old orchard grow on sloping ground. Falling white flakes have added another layer to the blanket of snow which fell two days before. A purposeful line of prints marks the passing of a predatory fox. On the far side of the trees the red-brown shape stands knee deep in snow. Pointed ears twitch and the head turns

Gale-blown, bare, twisted branches encrusted with lichen growth are the backdrop to an orchard seen in spring. The short, cropped grass and the browsed line of the trees show that cattle have grazed here in the recent past

towards the ground, straining to catch the sound of unseen prey. A quick arching pounce buries its face, then another short leap and the fox emerges with a mouthful of snow and a meal. Beneath that icy layer lies a series of runs – tiny snowbound passageways made by the field vole in the grass.

Festooning wintry branches, lichens thrive only where the air is unpolluted. Undisturbed for many years these extraordinary, ancient and slow growing plants adorn the oldest trees. Epiphytic in nature, lichens do not invade the tissues of their hosts, gaining only a vantage point from which to grow; a growth which occurs mainly in the cold season before the leaves of the apple trees shade the branches and ground below. But, while lichens do little real damage to the trees, it is doubtful whether a parasite that invades the living structure would have been allowed to survive, were it not for a pagan custom. The mistletoe is to many a mysterious plant, steeped in history and legend; found worldwide in many different forms it is represented in Britain by only one species. Commonly found on the continent, vast quantities are imported from Normandy for Christmas celebrations. As old orchards become increasingly rare, so too does the mistletoe, for despite being found on a few other trees, the apple is the most common host. Although not just confined to orchards, mistletoe was once

74

believed to improve the yield of fruit and as such its presence was tolerated and at times even actively encouraged. Growing in a ball of green branches and leaves it bears white berries in winter. Only a few birds are attracted to the fruit; mainly thrushes, with perhaps the occasional wintering waxwing, take advantage of the festive crop, despite its gluelike consistency. It is therefore ironic that in the past the berries were used by trappers to make birdlime – the seeds catching the very birds which helped them scatter. For although birds do wipe mistletoe seeds onto branches after a meal, most are sown in their droppings. A mistle thrush can pass a seed in the amazingly short time of thirty minutes and so it is hardly surprising that the distribution of the mistletoe is locally common.

Once fixed to a branch by the remains of its hardening flesh, the seed produces a strange type of root which defies botanical description – perhaps a combination of rhizome and root. The first small green growth clamps even tighter on the bark and the haustorium root then invades the conductive tissues of its involuntary host, tapping its nutrient source. Each year of the mistletoe's growth is marked by a fork in its branch and the tiny almost insignificant unisexual flowers are sometimes borne on separate plants. Although its pollen is spread by the wind, in early spring its nectar is a vital nourishment for honeybees and flies, which could also aid its pollination.

Bearing brilliant white berries in mid winter the mistletoe is an attractive parasitic plant favouring apple and poplar trees. Its fruit and flowers offer seasonal sustenance to birds and bees

TOAD IN THE HOLE

An autumn gale had brought more than a windfall to an orchard as one of the trees had blown to the ground, revealing a hole and the remains of an old bird's nest inside. Damaged in the fall the nest chamber had been partly exposed and so provided an ideal chance to see within the tree. Sealed and propped back up, the site was left for vacant possession.

Late the following spring a pair of blue-tits built a new feather-lined nest of dry moss. Filming proceeded and eventually five young eventually fledged and successfully left the nest. By summer's end the orchard had been deserted by breeding birds and an inspection of the hole was made to clear out any old nesting material. The entrance stood at about eye level from the ground and so would have contained only a few beetles and the odd slug or snail. But the biggest surprise was a large fat toad squatting in the remains of the moss.

The leaning trunk would have been fairly easy to climb and an acrobatic amphibian could have swung down and into the hole, yet what possessed a toad to go tree climbing will probably remain one of the secrets of nature.

The mistle thrush is a bird of the woodland edge and areas of open country, scattered with trees, and as such it has taken readily to farms and country gardens. Named in the past after what was thought to be its staple winter diet, it is now known to feed as much on earthworms as on fruits and berries. The largest and boldest of the thrushes, its loud ringing song can be heard in January even in the teeth of a howling winter gale. Long before the first leaves appear the mistle thrush has laid its eggs high up in the fork of an apple tree. The birds are now at their most aggressive, not feigning an attack on a passing cat or any other threat – and that includes mankind. Feeding on insects as well as larvae pulled from the orchard grass, a mistle thrush pair usually manages to rear two broods of four young each year. Once fledged they leave the orchard for more open ground.

Where rotted wood has formed a cavity in an old apple tree or where woodpeckers have been practising their art, other birds soon exploit the hole for a nest. Not much larger than a sparrow, the lesser-spotted woodpecker is surprisingly small. Its quiet drumming high up on slender branches and its soft calls make it less conspicuous than its greater cousin. Boring into decaying wood this energetic bird produces small-entranced nests for other birds in subsequent years. Its comparative rarity combined with its small size and quiet habits means that it is seldom seen, but orchards are known to be favoured places.

Blue tits are versatile birds found almost everywhere there are trees. The inside of apple boughs are among the many nooks and crannies they will occupy to rear their young. Starlings too will take over any hole large enough to accommodate their broods. But apart from tiny woodpeckers and large bold thrushes, the only other bird found with any regularity in the orchard is the goldfinch. Wherever there are thistles and other suitable seed-producing weeds, the goldfinch will not be far away. Its nest can be found high in the branches of an apple tree or sometimes in the surrounding hedge. Indeed so

Opposite: The mistle thrush is today a familiar bird of the orchard and one of the first to breed, often well before the apple blossom breaks. But it was once a shy bird of mountains over much of Europe before changing in recent times to living closer to man (*Photo: Roger Hosking*)

securely anchored is it with spiders' web that in winter the deserted deep cup shape can still be seen, swaying in the wind.

The bullfinch is another hedge-nester; but earlier in the year, when the blossom has still to break, these spectacularly coloured birds can wreak havoc amongst the orchard's future crop. In some years, when other food is scarce, large flocks can herald disaster for the fruit grower by literally nipping the apples in the bud. A single pair however is unlikely to do much damage and, as the seasons advance, the birds will find other food more plentiful.

Lengthening days and growing warmth, the orchard in late spring can be an especially beautiful place. Bare branches sprouting the fresh green of new leaves are soon covered by pink-tinged white blossom. In just a few days a dramatic transformation marks the arrival of summer.

Bees are the most obvious insects at this time and for the fruit grower, one of the most important. Successful pollination is the key to a good crop and in many orchards beehives are introduced. The production of honey is an added bonus as the bees bustle amongst the blossom, carrying pollen from flower to flower. Honeybees are not the only orchard-dwelling pollinators. Many different types of larger bumblebees, tiny solitary bees and wasps, beetles and flies all play their part. Not all insects are as beneficial as the industrious army of pollinators and many consume more than the nectar intended to lure their kind. Consumed by legions of larvae, today's modern apple has inherited a host of harmful insects from its wild ancestral form. Even before the blossom has burst, the larva of the apple blossom weevil will eat the stamens and petals from within an unopened flower. Safe from foraging birds the only obvious sign is the wilted brown of the bud. The damage caused by this larval beetle is quite small and in many ways acts as a natural thinning agent for the later ripening fruit. Once it has eaten enough, the larva pupates before emerging as an adult – that is unless it is discovered by the only predator capable of detecting the grub: closely related to wasps and bees, ichneumon flies are a large group of insects that parasitize their prey. With its rapierlike ovipositor the fly probes inside the bud, laying its egg within the soft body of the imprisoned weevil grub.

From sooty blotch to silver leaf there are a variety of rots and moulds which attack the apple fruit and leaves. There is a continual onslaught of codling and winter moth caterpillars, capsid bugs and chafers, sawflies and spider mites, all intent on growing to the detriment of the tree. Yet it will survive, as it has for the past eighty years or more, to bear its autumn crop.

Between the trees stretches a carpet of undisturbed grass, unploughed since it was planted, perhaps centuries ago. Grazed by generations of sheep and sometimes cattle, many orchards now lie forgotten, neglected and knee-

Opposite: A fledgling blue tit surveys the outside world just before leaving its nest for the first and last time. Once flown it will follow its parents amongst the apple trees learning to search for food before beginning to fend for itself

HOME SWEET HOME

For more than forty centuries people have used an army of industrious workers to gather minute quantities of a rich and valuable crop. The honey-bee has been housed in purpose built structures, protected and bred all over the world. A warm weather creature thought to have originated in the east from India, their value is only out-weighed by their production of honey – an expensive luxury satisfying the human craving for sweetness and extensively used as a base for the brewing of alcoholic mead.

Foraging from dawn to dusk the honey-bees sensitivity to ultra-violet light leads it to the source of nectar. Favouring blue coloured flowers that are insect pollinated, the petals have honey guide lines only seen by sensitive eyes leading into its sweet centre. Finding their way to and from crops of fast flowing nectar by a simple form of solar navigation, even on cloudy days their ultra-violet vision can detect the position of the sun.

In Britain honey-bees are seldom found living in the wild as human made hives make ideal homes. Wax combs laden with sweet stores are readily removed by the bee-keeper who must ensure the safety of the colony by keeping harmful intruders at bay. Apart from two moths whose larvae feast on old combs and gouge channels in the wooden surround, one of the principal pests is the mouse.

The long-tailed or wood mouse spends the summer either out in the fields or around the woods. A strikingly marked rodent of considerable agility thay can jump surprising distances. In the autumn these mice often seek the shelter of farm buildings or any suitable structure. Their rounded shape belies the tiny gaps into which they can squeeze, especially under doors or bee hive entrances. Indeed so common is the problem that mouse guard mesh is fitted onto many hives.

It is only during cold weather when the bees are beginning to gather in preparation for the weeks of hibernation that the mice dare to enter the den of the well defended bees. In summer, when the colony is active and alert, any such intruder would be instantly attacked and re-pelled, and may even be stung to death. But in winter the dormant colony cluster together for warmth and safety between the hanging combs. It is as much the movement of the mice as the building of their leaf and grass lined nest as well as their nibbling holes in the wax, that disturbs the bees. The mouse may even consume any larvae still inside their cells and damage the honey store so vital to the over-wintering bees.

With the remains of the former residents littering the floor the mice set up home and may also begin to breed. A waterproof roof and insulated walls of wood protect the new rodent family from the elements as well as hunting cats. But the eventual return of warm, spring weather brings out the bee-keeper to check on the hives, and any unwelcome tenant is likely to be quickly evicted. To film such an event required not only a hive with some mice but someone willing to admit they were there. Placing an advertisement in a bee keepers' journal brought little in the way of response, as rodent residents are not considered good practice. The eventual location of a hive in which the birth of wild mice was watched, late one afternoon, was only filmed with one condition – not to tell the owner's name.

Uprooted by storm-force winds an old apple tree lies in a forgotten and neglected orchard. Visited only a few times a year when the crop is ready to be picked it's left alone to the wild for many months on end

deep in grass. Where uncut by man or four-legged mowers, this green matted meadow is ideal ground for the field vole to make its runs. Short-tailed, rounded and blunt-nosed, these small mammals create a maze of passageways just beneath the grassy jungle thatch. With an average life expectancy of little more than seven months, the reproductive rate of these rodents can, in a good year, be prodigious.

The field vole makes a nest of dried leaves, usually well hidden in a tussock of grass or in the hollowed base of an apple tree. From spring to autumn a succession of litters are born, each one containing up to six blind, naked and, at first, totally helpless young. Fast growing, they spend only three or four weeks in the nursery nest before leaving to establish their own territory of runs. From birth to breeding for the very first time, the life of the vole is in proportion to its size – short and fast.

As the principal prey of many mammals and birds the field vole plays an important part in the food chain. In years of plenty, when breeding is high, their numbers are reflected by the rearing success of kestrels and owls. Active, not just at their peaks of dawn and dusk, voles are hunted day and night. Feeding on the leaves and stems of grasses they forage along their runs and encounters between them can be clearly heard – loud chatterings coming from the grass.

Very little surpasses this scene on a warm evening in early June. Like a summer snowfall, waves of falling blossom drift across the orchard and the soft low light of the sun slants through the trees. On silent white wings a barn owl weaves between the branches, briefly hovering with rapid gentle strokes before continuing into the meadow beyond. Young rabbits grazing close to the hedge are startled and bolt for cover. Appearing once more, they hesitatingly hop to continue their nibbling feed, joined by more from the warren.

At the far end of the orchard, the leaning weathered timber of an old five bar gate contains more repair than original wood. Alongside, a small brown shape is often to be found perched on the equally ancient post. For the little owl the orchard is a regular haunt and its nest is sometimes made in the base of a hollow trunk — a tree that was originally planted towards the end of the last century when the little owl was still a stranger to British shores. Its subsequent success and spread was undoubtedly due as much to the availability of its mainly insect and earthworm food, as to the number of suitable orchards and parklands. But the prey of this diminutive yellow-eyed owl is not just confined to the boneless; it also catches small mammals, birds, frogs and lizards. Though most active in twilight at the beginning and end of day it will also hunt into the night. The little owl is the smallest and most

From the base of an apple tree stump a little owl peers intently with yellow gleaming eyes. The most active of all owls during the day it feeds mainly on insects and other small prey rather than mammals and birds

common day-flying owl in the countryside. And with its conspicuous bounding flight and curious bobbing when approached, it is also easily recognised.

Almost as quickly as blossom coloured the barely leafed trees, its falling signals the passing of spring. Growing leaves increase the orchard's shade and the continual frantic hum of a million insect wings gradually fades, to be replaced by the sounds of summer – the strident tones of grasshoppers mix with the mewing call of a buzzard in a cloudless sky. From the hedge comes the exploding song of a wren. And the hungry twittering of a blue tit family sounds from the branches of a tree, their pale plumage blending with the green hue of apple leaves.

Still air and a heavy dew soak the orchard at dawn and the coolness of early day gives way to the growing strength of the sun. Against an earth bank an old pile of dung, covered with grass cuttings, has lain for the past year. Lit by a shaft of light in the gently rising steam, the coiled olive-scaled shape of a grass-snake basks in the sun. Although the largest native serpent found in Britain, the grass-snake is completely harmless. Extremely shy and consequently seldom seen, its size can be a surprise. Adult females have been known to reach nearly 2m (6ft) in length, but just over half that size is more the norm. In contrast the male is smaller still and rarely reaches 80cm (31.5in) from reptile head to scaly tail. The snake's most distinctive mark, apart from an olive green or brown colour and a series of dark bars streaked down each side, is a pale yellow collar. Bordered in black and lying just behind the head it is a feature, along with the snake's size, that distinguishes it from the venomous adder.

Seeking out a warm moist place, the female grass-snake lays from ten to more than forty eggs, though the larger snakes tend to lay the most eggs. Compost heaps and dung piles are the most sought-after reptilian nurseries. Once laid, the eggs and newly hatched young are on their own although some females may remain nearby for a few days. Beneath the rising mist of decay and incubated by the warmth of rotting vegetation, the eggs are deposited in clusters held together by a mucus that eventually dries. White and leathery skinned, the eggs differ from those of birds as they have been developing for some time before being laid. Continuing to take up water, they expand in size and, around the end of August, depending on the incubating temperature, the young snakes begin to emerge. From a split in the egg a glistening green little head with a flicking forked tongue appears. For a few hours it remains safe inside, just its tongue tasting the air, finally emerging in a long line of effortless ease. Within the next twelve hours the baby snake sheds the egg tooth which helped make good its escape.

Where suitable sites are few and far between, several female snakes may

Opposite: The adaptable ever present blue tit can be found almost everywhere providing there are trees, not only with holes for nesting but as a source of caterpillar food for their young (*Photo: Roger Hosking*)

THE EDIBLE MOUSE

From a Roman recipe in the first century A.D. comes the description of a fashionable delicacy. Just as wine has its devotees so too did the squirrel-tailed or edible dormouse. Perhaps originally introduced by the Romans, today's population stems from those released from a Hertfordshire park at Tring around 1902. Native to southern and eastern Europe, these bushy-tailed, large grey mice are often found around orchards. Mainly nocturnal and feeding on fruits, as well as insects and nuts, they are agile climbers spending most of their lives up in trees.

The Romans once waxed lyrical about its taste, but in the years that followed its English release complaints of damage to corn crops and thatch proved it to be more of a pest. During winter the edible dormouse hibernates, sometimes in a social nest containing several curled up and sleeping grey mice. But it's in the autumn that most of the damage is done. As they are found frequently in close association to man, the mouse enters barns and sheds in search of its favourite food. For unlike its European relatives it seldom takes fruit from the trees, preferring to raid stores of apples even in the grower's own home.

lay in the same heap, producing a considerable collection of eggs, at times numbering into the hundreds. The young newly hatched snakes may then remain within the heap or seek out other places to hide, usually underground. Hibernating during the cold winter months, young snakes can apparently live without eating from first hatching to spring, when those which survive emerge to feed for perhaps the very first time.

Long since pruned, the lengthening apple branches reaching for the sky are now beginning to bend beneath the growing weight of the crop. Beauty of Bath, Bramley and Kingston Black, the named varieties and the quantity of apples once seemed almost as endless as the orchards that contained them. Cookers and eaters for the farmhouse kitchen were also a source for the cider industry. Now almost forgotten, the fruits of the orchard ripen in the late summer sun, and a new wave of wildlife takes advantage of this free food left hanging around.

Wasps arrive in ever-increasing numbers. Enlarging a hole first pecked by a bird, workers and drones eat into its very core. When damaged by birds, apples are readily infected by the airborne spores of rots and moulds which are also carried from fruit to fruit by marauding wasps. Living up to its name, the brown rot fungus begins as a small dark patch which quickly grows as the rot invades the apple's flesh. Pathetic, brown and shrivelled the fruit may hang on the trees for some considerable time.

Other members of the rot world are not quite so obvious and first consume the apple from within before showing their true colours on the skin. Falling to the orchard floor, the soft rotting remains of the apple attract another more handsome insect. Red admiral butterflies, feasting in profusion on the fermenting juices of the festering fruit, are common in early autumn. They are peculiar insects, for they are still common despite their inability to survive a British winter. The answer lies to the south, for across from the continent a mass migration arrives each spring. Millions of brightly winged insects fly north from coast to coast, and lay eggs to produce a large British-born population of red admiral caterpillars that consume vast quantities of stinging nettles.

In late summer the first native red admiral butterflies take wing. Then, incredibly, their numbers are swollen by a further mass migration from the continent. As days become shorter, summer temperatures wane and the night air rapidly cools, the red admirals begin to disappear from view, and despite their search for safe winter quarters, few if any will survive to see a British spring. Certain individuals appear not to share the same winter fate; emerging after August, they show a reverse tendency in their general flight direction and head south, as do other individuals over much of continental Europe.

This spectacular annual movement is a feature shared with another and perhaps even more remarkable long-distance traveller. The painted lady butterfly can, in some years, be seen feeding on the orchard's fallen fruit. Its life cycle is also marked by massive seasonal migrations involving millions of insects worldwide. Carried on fragile coloured wings, the aptly-named painted lady, steadily flying north in March and April, arrives in Europe from North Africa. In the autumn the pattern is again reversed by a successive generation and it once more returns to wintering grounds, south of the Mediterranean.

The migration of European butterflies is seldom as spectacular or impressive as the en masse movement of the North American monarchs or

A perfect miniature of the adult, a newly hatched grass snake remains for a while near the other leathery-skinned eggs before slipping easily into the cover of its rotting nursery heap where it may remain all winter

Deep inside a dry grass nest young field voles are naked, blind and helpless at little more than one day old, yet within a few weeks they will be weaned and starting to become independent and making their own series of runs

the exotic butterflies of the tropics, but in terms of distance they are more than a match. Over much of Britain and the continent, careful observation has revealed a steady stream of butterflies, at certain times of the year – a movement which is neither random nor entirely infrequent but more an annual episode of life.

The changing season is shown by the altered colour of apple leaves and dew-laden spiders' webs. The cool freshness of autumnal days is as much a contrast to the muggy warmth of summer as the growing redness of the fruit. A breeze stirs the upper branches of a heavily laden tree and the first of the winter windfall begins. Rising in the east, a nearly full moon looks strangely out of place in a pale blue sky. But on the opposite horizon a setting sun is not so much the end of another day as the beginning of another night – a time of activity for nocturnal life. Voles move out from the cover of their runs to feed on the windfall fruit, while on the far side of the orchard nearest the wood, a large dark shape comes through the hedge, on a well worn path. Sweet apples and, especially, small succulent pears are relished by badgers. A combined family of seven is not unusual in some orchards at night. Made up of more than one litter they raid the fruit in a group, their outlines clearly seen by the light of the moon. The badger is surprisingly omnivorous and windfalls in season provide an easy meal.

At first light the silence which has remained almost unbroken for the past few weeks is shattered. The increasing clamour comes from a flock of hungry starlings as they descend upon the orchard. Throughout most of Britain and Ireland the winters are relatively mild when compared to the freezing winds of central and northern Europe. British starlings are almost entirely residential, remaining within these shores. But eastward across the continent the winters become increasingly severe and the starlings more migratory. In eastern Europe the entire population of these birds flies south and west for the snowbound months of the year. Flocking together, resident and migrant starlings scavenge the countryside in search of food. Song thrushes and even blackbirds will migrate from the severity of a hard winter in northern Europe.

Fleeing before the advancing snows come other Scandinavian birds. Flocks of redwings and fieldfares often fly in by night. Their flight calls maintain contact within the flock and are the only sounds which betray their passing, somewhere in the darkness overhead. The redwing is the smallest of the thrushes found in Britain, and along with the larger fieldfares it feeds on the orchard windfall. For these birds, apples are often the only source of food in the freezing landscape of midwinter. In bad years thousands of birds are forced to fly in the face of advancing blizzards in northern Britain. In the

Imbibing the juices of over-ripe fruit red admiral butterflies are often to be found in the late summer orchard. Cool and full of fermented apple they can be approached quite closely as they indulge in their annual feast

When windfalls leave a surplus of food scattered across the grass, rotting fruit can attract a larger relative of wasps. The hornet is not as aggressive as its reputation but is equally partial to apples

southwest, old orchards in Devon and Somerset provide short-term sustenance during the worst of the weather.

As the apples are eaten or hidden by fresh falls of snow, competition for the remaining fruit becomes fierce. Redwings compete noisily for the same apples and even challenge fieldfares with some success, but they are no match for the starlings – noisy, aggressive birds that dominate these frantic gatherings. Chaffinches, too, join the flocking feasters in the orchard but, being smaller still, they remain in the wings of the drama, ready to dart in and pick the pips from the exposed apple cores. With the coming thaw the birds disperse into the surrounding country, continuing to feed on wild hedgerow fruit, earthworms and insect larvae in the pastures. And as winter once more retreats to the north so too do the surviving birds.

The mistle thrush heralding the spring perhaps also heralds the disappearance of the orchard from the farm. Once the farmer's family would collect to gather the ripened crop and on the traditional farm many apples, having dropped in the grass, would still be left to the wild. But in an old neglected orchard where the fruit remains untouched by human hand, it is nature that reaps the short-term benefit. The apples left to fall are plundered by the wildlife feasting on the fruits of man's neglect.

When winter wind and cold has claimed the last of the deciduous leaves a few apples may remain on some types of trees, along with a leafy ball of green. The mistletoe remains hidden for much of the year, comes into its own when all else is laid bare

5 THE HAZEL COPSE

Rain dripping from colourful autumn leaves soaks the woodland floor below. Beneath a canopy of fading green, with its aroma of damp earth and rotting leaves, the still air and muted sounds could be the setting for a prehistoric scene. Set apart from the rest of the world by a wall of standing wood, the copse today can seem to be a million miles from the rest of the farm. A greenwood ark that has carried plants and animals into the present day can permeate a timeless quality – a relic of ancient forests that belies its tree-planted nature. Of all the trees in the greenwood the hazel not only holds the key to the copse, but has the fruits for its and others' survival.

As autumn plenty gives way to the leaner days of winter, the copse is isolated still further by the unearthly quiet of falling snow. Bare hazel branches slowly bend beneath the weight of a white layer and a crystal blanket envelops the trees. In the days which follow, animal tracks left in the snow read like a diary of recent events. The straight-lined trail of a passing fox crosses the ambling ploughed track of a badger. And on the woodland edge a mass of rabbit prints overlain by those of a fox, freshly excavated earth, tufts of fur and scattered drops of blood, write the drama of a fox's meal in the snow. Beneath the covering of snow the woodmouse has a series of underground runs with a hidden store of hazelnuts, to survive the worst of the winter's icy cold. Yet, even when the ground is covered with snow, the mouse will still forage at night, leaving a telltale trail to its underground home – a network of tight passageways excavated between the roots of a hazel. Safe from all but the smallest of predators, the woodmouse is a favoured prey of the weasel. Its tiny sinuous body negotiating mouse holes with ease, the weasel will penetrate deep below ground in search of its rodent quarry. Re-emerging into the white winter landscape, the weasel briefly stands upright investigating the surrounding country, before bounding off in the curious undulating gait of its family.

Opposite: Tightly curled the dormouse survives the cold winter months in a sleep, a state of suspended animation that conserves its vital fatty stores laid down beneath its skin, enough to survive up to half a year without feeding

Small mammals have evolved many different strategies to survive the cold months of the year. Unlike woodmice and voles which remain active throughout the seasons, the dormouse eats its fill in autumn and hibernates the winter through – and that's why it was once known as the hazel sleeper. Remaining within its tight-balled nest of finely stripped honeysuckle bark, it leaves no trail for predators to follow, but if found by chance fast asleep, it would be an easy picking.

The hibernation nest itself is usually made at or below ground level, sometimes even in the cleft of a tree base. Surrounded by fallen leaves it looks no different to any other woodland litter, save for the furry bundle hidden inside. The dormouse increases its fat reserves by feasting on nuts and berries in early autumn. Rapidly gaining in weight this pot-bellied little rodent can appear almost spherical. Sealing its nest so no entrance remains, the dormouse then prepares for its long cold sleep. Tucking its head into its stomach, screwing up its eyes and wrapping its soft furry tail up and over its head, it descends into a deep winter sleep. As it drifts into a state of dormancy, its body heat slowly ebbs away. Breathing is shallow and irregular and its heartbeat slows to a remarkably low rate – like its breathing, barely discernible. Muscles stiffen with the cold and the body remains just above freezing. In this state of suspended animation, the special brown fat store laid down within the body provides the essential food to maintain the reduced bodily processes; enough to last for months.

Although hibernation usually lasts from October through to April, it is not entirely continuous. A few days of activity appear to be alternated with several weeks of sleep. The onset of hibernation is thought to be triggered as much by the accumulation of body fat as by the dropping of the surrounding temperature. Severe cold, however, can have the reverse effect, for if the body is in danger of being frozen alive, the animal stirs and shivers – producing heat within the muscles and so raising its temperature a few life-giving degrees. If the intense cold continues the dormouse may even wake completely, consuming far more of its valuable fatty stores as it moves around within the nest. A slight warming of the weather thaws the frozen ground and once more the dormouse can lapse into winter torpor.

In the lengthening days of February hazel catkins slowly unfurl, releasing clouds of yellow pollen into the air. These flamboyant straggling tails, adorning the tree's bare branches, are the male parts of the hazel flower. In contrast the tiny red stigma of the female flower are small and incon-spicuous, easily overlooked, even on the same branch. A fertile yellow dust carried on the wind, means that pollination for the hazel is as much by chance as by evolved design. Overgrown and neglected for years, stout hazel branches radiate up from the base – a sure sign of a once-coppiced wood.

Opposite: The hazel copse in winter reveals the tall straggling limbs of a once coppiced wood with year old growth beyond. Covered in snow with more beginning to fall the woodland is blanketed in silence

Blown by a breath of cold wind millions of pollen grains are released by hazel catkins early in the year. A cloud carried by chance to the tiny female flowers that will bear the hazel nuts

But where still coppiced, the clearings increase the woodland edge – an area containing a far greater diversity and wealth of life than the sun-shaded dark interior of a midsummer copse.

The amount of sunlight reaching the woodland floor profoundly affects the variety and abundance of wild flowers. Where man has recently laid his hand upon the wood of a copse, an even richer everchanging carpet of colour unfolds as the seasons progress. A profusion of bright yellow primroses yields some of the earliest blooms on south-facing banks. Here, too, the petals of celandine and the carpets of white wood anemone blossom and nod in the wind. Since they flower before the shade of growing leaves increases, these plants are able to grow in the shelter of broad-leaved woods. Towering above the hazel, oak trees were often planted with the coppice, and although adding another dimension to the diversity of these deciduous woods, they also cast a deeper shade. Eventually the growing leafy canopy becomes too dense for herbaceous plants to thrive, suppressed by the increasing gloom. So when the coppice is cleared there is a rush of vigorous growth. Dormant seeds germinate and flowers already growing are revitalised by the new-found light. Yellow archangel, bluebell and red campion follow in the wake of the primrose, all flourishing and fading in the seven year cycle of coppicing and growth.

An obvious animal in early spring is the alien grey squirrel indulging in its aerial antics. Running and leaping high in the trees it is easily seen without the cover of leaves. It is one of the earliest mammals to begin breeding and will sometimes commandeer a woodpecker's old hole. Deep inside the trunk of a tree the squirrel is comparatively safe from most predators, although the agile stoat can climb surprisingly well. The entrance to such a den is not as permanent as first appears – natural tree growth constantly constricts its size, and so the squirrel must continually gnaw at the hole to keep pace with the closing gap. Even the interior of a squirrel's newly found den must be enlarged to accommodate the birth of its litter. The young, as many as seven but more usually three, are nakedly defenceless at birth. Their distinctly ratlike appearance is a reminder of their rodent family. The nest chamber itself is lined to a considerable depth with soft material – grass, moss and even fur. Born helpless into the cold of a British spring the young need all the insulation the parent can provide. As the male plays no part in their upbringing, the female must leave them while she forages for food. For up to ten weeks the female will nurse her young before they finally leave the nest to explore their woodland world. Surprisingly long lived in captivity (up to twenty years is not unknown), they seldom survive more than eight or nine years in the wild. But considering that less than one in every hundred

The coppice floor in spring gives rise to early flowers; primrose, lesser celandine and the smaller sweet violet. The remains of a wood mouse's meal lies in a half gnawed shell while another unfound begins to grow

survives to the age of six, the mortality of those first few years is high indeed. Hunted by men and preyed upon by domestic cats and dogs, foxes, buzzards and even owls, it is perhaps surprising that grey squirrels are not only relatively common but that they survive at all.

As the seasonal progression of warmth and growth slowly extends from south to north, the deciduous woodlands of Britain awake to the songs of birds and a steadily advancing wave of colour. Along with the flowers and the bright green of fresh hazel leaves, are the tiny new clusters of primordial fruit. The growth of hazelnuts coincides with the emergence of a beetle from the dank earth beneath the leafy woodland floor. Tiny hazelnut weevils, with long protruding snouts, fly from ground to tree. The females seek out a soft growing nut and drill a neat little hole. A single egg is laid within and the continuing growth of the nut eventually seals the wound. Safe inside the hardening shell the tiny grub hatches from its egg and begins to consume the nut unseen. But it is not the only weevil to rely on this nut-bearing tree. In contrast to the dull brown of the hazelnut weevil is the striking bright red and black colour of the hazel leaf roller which gained its name from the way it rolls half a hazel leaf, as a nursery and food for its grub. It bites across from edge to centre on both sides of a leaf and leaves the midvein to support the hanging half. After laying a single egg, the weevil, using its tiny black legs,

Often one of the earliest mammals to breed in the new year is the introduced American grey squirrel. With eyes still yet to open they are left within their hollow tree-nest high off the ground

A bright red weevil crawling up its neatly curled nursery is the hazel leaf roller. Conspicuously coloured they are widespread if not particularly common and keep mainly to the canopy of leaves

carefully rolls the leaf. Feeding from within, the larva then consumes all but the outer layer before pupating. Eventually the outside may shrivel and brown and sometimes fall to the ground, from where the adult weevil will emerge, producing a second generation in the same season.

The increasing abundance of insect life and growing sheltered cover provide many different birds with sources of food and places to nest. The willow warbler is an attractive summer visitor, spending the winter months in Africa. Almost identical to the chiffchaff, the song is the only sure way of telling them apart. But while they both feed and nest in woodlands the chiffchaff tends to keep clear of the floor and the willow warbler lays its eggs at ground level so that its nest is always well concealed. The copse hums with life at this time of the year. From the early dawn chorus of birds, to the lazy buzzing of bumble bees and the sound of wind-rustled leaves there is constant background noise. On still days the clamour of animal life carries far as the drumming of a greater-spotted woodpecker echoes through the trees. It is a bird whose entire life is centred on the tree, as a place to resonate its hammering call as well as finding food beneath the bark. Hollowed out by the bird's chisel-like bill, a tree trunk becomes a secure place to raise its brood.

Lengthening shadows and a setting sun soon plunge the hazel wood into

dark, and the familiar sounds of daylight hours give way to the strange calls of night. Beneath the cloak of darkness a whole new world of wildlife is about – sometimes heard but seldom seen. It is a world we really know little about. A time when sounds and smell matter more than sight. For man, it is an unnatural hour, but in the woodlands of Britain many creatures emerge only at night. Warmer days bring shorter and warmer nights and the rising temperatures of late spring waken a winter sleeper; the dormouse has finally emerged from hibernation. Against the afterglow of a western sky, the speed and agility of these furry-tailed mice can just be seen. Leaping from tapering hazel branch to branch they chase each other in arboreal pursuit.

The summer nest of the dormouse is made above ground and, like the winter nest, is a ball of finely stripped honeysuckle bark entwined with occasional grass or moss. Hidden deep inside a dense clump of undergrowth, the nests are often protected by a tangle of nature's own barbed wire – the bramble. At first glance this compact round mass may be taken for a bird's nest, perhaps a wren's, but the absence of a clearly defined entrance is a sure sign of a dormouse home. They are strictly nocturnal, seldom, if ever, appearing by day. Climbing with remarkable agility through the shrub layer, they seek out their food of nuts, fruit, berries and buds. In early spring they may even take the occasional insect as well. The dormouse is the most attractive of all our native rodents, with large blackcurrant-like eyes, and beautiful dense chestnut coloured fur which is set off by a sweeping furry tail. They are generally silent, but the sound of shrill squeaking during pursuits has been heard.

If the dormouse is one of the smaller inhabitants of the copse after dark, then the badger is surely the largest. By the light of the moon the sight of that striped head emerging from the ground is enough to set the heart beating. By day, massive earthworks, mounds of soil thrown out in front of its hole are the badger's most obvious sign. Tons of earth accumulated over the seasons are a clue to the vast extent of the complex labyrinth of tunnels and chambers, which lie deep below the surface. The badger is the one animal that can actually alter the shape of the ground within the copse.

Many of the larger setts have a long history of use. Some have been occupied for hundreds of years by generation after generation of badgers. Old age is a luxury nature seldom affords in the wild and the average life expectancy for a newborn badger may be no more than two or three years. Rare is the adult which lives a decade or more. Well trodden paths radiating from a well used sett, and droppings in shallow pits dug a little way from the entrance, are sure signs of resident badgers.

Young badgers are born in early spring but are rarely seen above ground before they are two months old. The usual litter is of two or three. Where a

Opposite: The dormouse is an arboreal acrobat, agile and quite at home high in the trees leaping from branch to branch. Strictly nocturnal they are seldom if ever seen by day, more usually just a small, streaking silhouette against a darkening sky

copse is seldom disturbed badgers will emerge from their daytime retreat into the evening sun. In the soft light of sunset, early in May, the play of badger cubs is a delight to be seen and heard. Scuffling of leaves and a whickering noise, growls, runs and bumps are all part of the cubs' playful sounds. By three months of age that play is becoming quite boisterous, with 'king-of-the-castle' a popular game. Any mound, fallen tree or stump is commandeered by one cub, while the others attempt to dislodge the badger 'king'. Sometimes play will even begin before they leave the sett and sounds emanating from beneath the ground are a prelude to the evening's romp. The first badger out will sometimes turn and prevent the others from leaving, until in a final rush they tumble out in a heap. An important part of an animal's early days, play develops the skills and reflex speed needed for later life.

The badger is basically a forager, feeding on both plant and animal food. Its long sensitive snout noses the ground for hour after nocturnal hour seeking out its main tiny prey. Perhaps surprisingly, for a creature of its size, it is largely dependent upon the humble earthworm for its staple diet. Although they will and do eat most things which come their way, from fungi to frogs, birds, beetles, berries and rabbits, the larger prey is usually scavenged.

As darkness descends the badger cubs' play continues around the sett, for an hour or more. The adults will sometimes join in but more usually stay nearby. From out of the black a sudden loud piercing call cuts through the wood. Startled, the cubs hesitate for a moment, listening hard, before returning to their game, reassured by the lack of parental reaction. The call is that of a highly specialised avian hunter – the tawny owl is essentially a woodland bird. Sitting motionless on an overhead branch it will scan the woodland floor. Acute hearing and remarkably sensitive vision are just part of the tools of its trade. Silent flight is the essence of the nocturnal hunter, giving it the edge in the element of surprise. The tawny owl's large beguiling eyes belie its lethal nature. A faint, almost imperceptible, rustle of a leaf betrays its rodent prey. Eyes fix on the sound and the bird drops on silent outstretched wings.

Nesting inside the rotted trunk of an old oak, the female tawny will lay up to four round white eggs which rest on a soft bed of dry decaying wood and the debris of owl pellets. The female sits for hours, motionless except for the occasional glance towards the entrance hole if disturbed by a sound – it could be her mate returning with food. Standing up she stretches her legs and wings, fluffs her feathers and sits once more. Her vigil could last for nearly a month with only a few minutes away from the nest each night. Fed faithfully by the male, the female's real activity only begins after the hatch. Even then she remains brooding her young closely for the first few days.

Opposite: Soon after leaving the nest young tawny owls sit around awaiting the return of their parents. First flights often take them straight to the ground but using beak and claw they can readily climb back up again

HAMMERED HOME

Many different birds and mammals nest or hide in tree holes, but there is only one kind that can hammer a home out of wood. Where woodpeckers have chiseled a cavity other species can follow over subsequent years, especially if the hollow enlarges with rot. Nuthatches narrow the entrance by plastering with mud, which also makes a suitable size hole for a great tit. Both wrynecks and starlings will use cavities of similar dimensions but its not just birds that could gain access through such a hole. Dormice have been discovered in nest boxes put up originally for birds and so many use natural holes more often than is supposed. Bats are well known summer residents of tree hollows yet the stoat will also raise its family surprisingly high up a tree. More common and capable of enlarging the hole is the gnawing of the North American grey squirrel, and as the cavity grows in size larger birds like the stock dove or little owl will nest down inside. Tawny owls favour the roomier holes and even barn owls will move in if buildings are in short supply, but whatever the species the need for a secure hollowed tree remains the same to safely rear its young.

The owlets hatch as they were laid, one every forty-eight hours, so that their size reflects their age. The food, mainly mice and voles, is torn into pieces and fed to the young. But soon they, too, are swallowing shrews and small mice whole. After ten days the chicks have grown a dense covering of down and the female leaves them within an hour of dark. If the weather turns cold she may return to brood, but from now on the urgency is for food.

In a good year three chicks are usually reared and to feed them the adults must hunt late into the night. Woodmice, bank voles, shrews, even bats and frogs have been seen being fed to the ravenous young. Small birds, robins and sparrows are regular prey, as well as the occasional blackbird or even young jay. After such a meal the nest chamber is filled with floating feathers, as the adults tend to tear up this larger prey. Lifted by every flap of a wing, for several hours each parental arrival is greeted by a storm-stirred whirl of flying feathers. The young chicks sit with wide red-rimmed eyes, occasionally snapping at a passing plume. Jostling for the position nearest to the hole takes up much of their time. For that hole is the centre of their world, the direction for the arrival of food. Preening their growing plumage, and sleeping between feeds, takes up the rest of the night. Down below the foraging sounds of a family of badgers come and go in the night. A distant owl cry opens a sleeping eye but little else disturbs the chicks. A light pattering of

Still covered in down and hidden within a hollow tree, a pair of tawny owl chicks are too big to brood and so keep close together for warmth. They spend most of the day like this but more usually asleep

rain and the rustle of wind in the trees are the only other sounds to be heard.

A most extraordinary sight to witness came with the return of the male one night. The bird was carrying some rodent prey, which, as it was swallowed by a chick, was identified as a dormouse by the long furry tail. A chance event which is probably a unique record of a tawny owl taking this rare and endangered mouse. Although dormouse remains have been found in an owl pellet, it appears that this was the first time the actual feeding to a chick had ever been seen. As if that were not remarkable enough, the adult owl returned on subsequent nights with fish. Again, from bones found at other nest sites, it would seem that tawny owls do take fish, but here was conclusive proof in its beak. The owl's underfeathers were still quite wet, as were those around the lower half of its face, suggesting the fish was caught in some shallows. A possible source was a stream, only a few seconds' flight away. And as tawny owls regularly bathe, fish was probably a regular meal. Later identified as a bullhead, it is a fish which shuns the day, only becoming active at night. Swimming and feeding in shallow water, it would be a tempting target for a night bathing owl.

By midnight all the owlets have been fed and, with appetites replete, their incessant clamouring becomes more subdued when a parent returns with

Young roe deer like their parents are shy and wary animals with the senses of sight, sound and especially smell remarkably acute. Keeping to cover by day, clearings and woodland edge are only grazed during darkness, dawn and dusk

The many legs of a millipede making light work of climbing over a leaf is only one of millions of tiny animals in a handful of woodland litter. The life of the copse continues as much under foot as it does up in the trees

food. The chicks are then left alone, until hunting resumes once more in the early hours before dawn giving a final meal which sees the chicks through the long inactive hours of day. After five weeks the near full-grown owls leave the security of the nest. At first they spend hours peering from the entrance hole, watching the outside world. Tufts of soft downy feathers, lightly covering the cryptic brown of the adult plumage, help them still to retain their juvenile appearance. For the following three months they will continue to demand parental attention with their urgent hunger calls. Scattered throughout the woods, they hide by day, high up close to the trunk of a tree. By night the adults feed them one by one until eventually the young leave and establish territories of their own.

As the crescendo of the dawn chorus begins to die in the increasing morning light, a movement on the woodland edge reveals the halting, twitching-eared shape of a tiny deer. A roe deer, half hidden in dappled woodland shade, neatly strips hazel leaves from one twig at a time. Feeding at dawn and dusk in the open, these deer return to cover during the day. Being basically solitary, they seldom form herds, except occasionally in winter. But in summer groups of just a few may graze together. Bramble leaves are an important part of their yearly diet and in summer the broad leaves of hazel, oak and ash are browsed extensively.

A Bird's Eye View

At more than two houses high the nest of one of Britain's largest birds of prey had been built high up in a tree, where a platform of twigs and leaves supported a growing brood of buzzards. Far away the adults' mewing cry could be heard as they hunted the slopes, soaring on the day's first thermals. Back at the nest their three young chicks were unaware of being watched. Four ladders up and lashed between two boughs a green canvas hide and secure wooden floor gently swayed with the tree. Equipment and cameras were pulled up from the ground and when finally left alone the only sound came from passing insects and song birds using the hide as a perch.

The oak stood tall in a hillside wood and from beneath its new green canopy the view stretched far beyond. The parent birds returned to feed their young but seldom stayed more than a few minutes. As the sun slipped away from the wood someone returned to see me out, and the realisation of nine cramped and confined hours meant a stiff-legged descent to the ground, and yet another day in the life of a buzzard.

For many creatures the hazel copse is a sheltered home from which forays into the surrounding country can be made. The fox is no exception, and when it comes to breeding it will often seek out disused rabbit holes or abandoned badger setts in the cover provided by a copse. If the fox excavates its own earth it is not as complex or extensive as a badger's. The earth is occupied by the female for the birth of her young and for a few weeks more, otherwise adults prefer to lie up in dense cover above ground.

Emerging at dusk to hunt for small mammals, the fox is an opportunist when it comes to food, taking almost any prey which comes its way. It is, however, more likely to be seen by day than many other woodland dwellers. Young foxes playing outside their den can be encountered late into the morning. A handful of four cubs plaguing the life out of their mother is an entertaining sight, as they hang on to her tail and take playful bites at ears and feet. The cubs are generally completely preoccupied with their games, but it is rare to see an adult not completely alert. With acute senses far more sensitive than our own, the fox melts into the surrounding cover at the slightest hint of danger.

In the vibrant warmth of summer the strong colours of the red campion can only be found outside the shaded wood, around the edge and in the coppiced clearings. Bluebells that once carpeted the floor are now almost over as the fully grown hazel leaves cast their deepest shadow. In turn these leaves become a staple food for an army of caterpillars, munching on their stomachs. An astonishing array of size and colour, they grow and eat for the most part where they were laid, or descend from the oak canopy above. Dropping down on silken threads they reach the tender new growth of hazel leaves. Yet despite the number and variety of caterpillars which consume its foliage, few are exclusive to the hazel alone.

Opposite: The juvenile greater-spotted woodpecker wears a distinctive red crown. These birds are often architects and builders for a long line of subsequent home owners, as only the woodpecker can excavate a hollow from a solid wood trunk

The nut tree tussock is the only moth which takes its name from the tree. And besides a number of even smaller ones, looking more like clothes moths, over thirty different large moth caterpillars are known to eat hazel leaves. Winter moth and mottled umber, two of the greatest oak defoliators, are also partial to hazel. Lobster, buff tip, pale tussock, coxcomb prominent, lackey, green silver-lines and large emerald as well as clouded magpie are just a few of the descriptively-colourful names of leaf-consuming caterpillars.

Robustly armoured green shield bugs squat amongst the foliage and, lurking in the greenery, the aptly named click beetle has the disconcerting habit, if touched, of disappearing with a surprisingly loud click.

High above the woodland canopy the mewing cry of a buzzard echoes across the valley. The largest of our common birds of prey, the buzzard will circle for hours on warm currents of air. It is a hunter which is literally at the top of the predatory tree; rabbits from around the woodland edge form an important part of its daily diet, especially when rearing young. In the topmost branches of an oak, some considerable distance even above the hazel, the buzzard has its nest. A tangle of large twigs, securely seated in a fork, supports the ungainly brood of three. Covered in white down they huddle together in the shallow cradle of their lofty platform – a nest which gives them an outstanding view over the rest of the farm. After two or three hours a parent's returning cry may only raise a wary eye from one of the chicks. But with a flap of huge brown wings, the parent's arrival back at the nest is greeted with a frantic commotion. Large prey such as rabbits are usually torn to pieces and fed to the largest, loudest and most persistent chick, the rest of the brood not getting a chance as outsize claws and stubby wings keep them at bay. Once the oldest chick has been fed, the others take their turn. And any remains of the meal are left on the side of the nest, a convenient snack for a hungry brood to nibble between main meals.

The parents gone once more, the chicks shuffle about their arboreal home, picking and peering at anything that takes their interest. Every so often one will move from the safety and security of the centre and reverse towards the edge. Backing carefully up to the perimeter of the nest and raising its stumpy tail, it squirts a white jet of faecal remains out into the copse. In a dry summer with little or no rain to wash the wood, the white-splattered leaves of the surrounding hazel begin to signpost the nest above.

As the buzzard chicks steadily grow, the parents allow the youngsters to tear up their own meals. Learning from practical experience they can soon deal with the largest of prey. For up to fifty days they remain in the nest before beginning to follow their parents' lead in the daily hunt for food. An aerial search which quarters the ground relies upon their remarkable vision.

Opposite: In early spring the woodland floor may hide the germinating future of a new hazel tree. Yet few will survive, nibbled by mice and rabbits, for wild grown hazel is surprisingly rare as most have been coppiced sometime in the past

FOOD FOR THOUGHT

Familiar to so many but watched by very few the tawny owl is a bird about which surprisingly little is known. Its nocturnal habit and ferocious reputation has helped to retain its secret nature. Hunting begins soon after dark, as during the day the sight of an owl sends small birds into a combined mobbing attack. Their reaction is not however unfounded as the tawny will even take blackbirds at night.

Regurgitating a pellet of undigestible fur and bones, owls produce a packet of information revealing their daily diet. Occasionally one discovery may lead to another, as when dormouse bones were found in an area much further north than where the mammals were previously known to live. The finding of fish bones had pointed in the past to perhaps a scavenged meal, but when a tawny owl returned to its nest carrying a fish the proof was seen in the eating. Both bullhead and stone loach are nocturnal fish found in shallow streams, a tempting target for these regularly bathing owls. Fishing may also explain why a tawny owl was seen peering into a garden goldfish pond, now there is food for thought.

With a raucous cry and bright blue wing flashes the jay is a watchful bird that seldom allows a close approach. Collecting nuts and acorns they bury a large number each year of which only a few are retrieved

Rabbits will form a large part of their prey when in sufficient numbers, but buzzards are not averse to taking the tiniest of quarry, even as small as a beetle. Sitting on a low branch well within the copse, they can even be seen alongside a flight path, conveniently cleared as a woodland walk, patiently watching and waiting for small mammals or even a worm.

From the upper storey of oak to the hazel and flowering herbs the life of the copse all eventually comes to earth. The leaves begin to fall. In the soft damp layers of the woodland floor decomposition begins. Bacteria, moulds and fungi work unceasingly, breaking down the leaf litter, and the life that was once the woodland's colour becomes part of the soil. Yet amongst the decay of previous years an entire animal community flourishes. Wood-boring beetles weaken the largest timber and fungi then does the rest. Carnivorous centipedes scour the jungle of rotting leaves in search of their tiny prey, while the harmless many-legged millipede feeds only on the decaying vegetation.

These in turn become food for a voracious little hunter. One of the most active of mammals is only of fractional size. The common shrew, smaller than a mouse, hunts almost continually for its carnivorous diet. Bustling with bursts of activity, day and night, it forages along regular shrew-size runs.

In the early days of autumn the foxgloves' flowering spikes have already

113

turned to seed and the trumpets of honeysuckle flowers hang withered from a bough, its twining stem using the hazel as support. The flowers of the honeysuckle were a nectar source for long-tongued night-flying moths. Even its leaves provided food for the dormouse after dark, and fine-frayed bark left hanging in long strips shows signs of its handiwork.

The larvae of the white admiral butterfly also eat honeysuckle leaves, spinning a suspended cocoon and emerging as adults late in the summer. The caterpillars feeding openly on the leaves by day make no attempt to hide. Nature has devised a remarkable way to disguise their vulnerable bodies by attaching pellets of their own droppings onto their backs with silk — a camouflage which resembles a fragment of debris rather than a morsel for a bird. In autumn the caterpillar weaves a winter cocoon by spinning a honeysuckle leaf to a twig. Safe inside this silk and leaf shelter it passes the coldest months, emerging briefly to feed on the new growth of leaves, for just a few weeks in the spring.

Throughout the year many animals have reaped the benefits of food and shade in the hazel copse, and September is the time when the wood begins to yield the fruits of summer. Hazelnuts, now full size, turn from creamy white to pale brown and the wildlife of the wood takes advantage of the season's crop. An arboreal acrobat hanging from its hind feet reaches for the furthest fruit — the grey squirrel gorges on ripening hazelnut clusters. Grasping a nut in its paws it nimbly turns it around and with one quick bite splits the shell in half. Its technique for dealing with hard-shelled nuts is one that grows with age. Young squirrels take much longer to reach the kernel of their desire. Older and wiser, mature squirrels are more experienced and deal with each nut in just a few seconds.

Bits and pieces of hazelnut shell litter the ground below a squirrels' feast. Discarding apparently empty nuts they let them fall to the floor. And it is now that the grub of the weevil makes its escape. For the past few months it has gorged unseen inside the developing fruit. Fully mature, the grub gnaws a neat hole through the surrounding shell. Wriggling out of the nursery nut it burrows into the loose leafy soil and pupates. Passing the winter under-ground, the adult hazelnut weevil digs to the surface in spring and flies to the nearest tree.

Fungi, fed by the richness of rotted leaves, seem to spring up from the soil overnight. The seasonal colours of the shortening days have quickly spread across the country scene, as the surrounding farm prepares for winter. The loud raucous call of a jay scolds a passing squirrel and showers of yellowed leaves fall with each breath of wind. Unhindered by millions of leaves a cold breeze begins to blow through the copse.

The bright blue-winged flashes of the jay are conspicuous in the fall as they

Opposite: The silver washed fritillary is one of the largest butterflies to be seen in the wood, flying in sunlit glades. Its rich orange background colour and dark chequered markings make it a conspicuous sight from early spring through to the summer

THE NATIVE NUT

Digging down through the soil is to travel backwards in time as layers of decomposed growth steadily add to the depth. Pollen grains from centuries past reveal not only the years of that growth but the type and variety of trees. From Irish sites the amount of hazel pollen reaches up to seventeen times the total of other tree pollen, and up to four times in England. Indeed to travel back in time eight thousand years might have found a woodland floor covered in fallen fruit, for that was when vast hazel groves produced an abundance of nuts. Today the remnants of such stands are only found in the hills of the Lake District, western Scotland and lush remote valleys of Ireland's County Clare.

The hazel perhaps first spread from nuts that floated north, on the rivers Seine and Rhine. Carried by birds or squirrels, even stone age man, pigs might have swallowed some whole and beavers carried entire branches. Once established it spreads by seeds and suckers. As the only native edible nut-bearing tree, perfect for coppicing growth, it's not surprising it was put to such good use by generations of people, and so to find a naturally growing untouched tree is today almost a rarity.

collect, eat and bury nuts. They are a menace to many birds in summer, when eggs and young of songsters are regularly in their diet. In autumn their attention turns to a more vegetarian kind of food – acorns and hazelnuts – which are often swallowed whole. A different tactic is adopted by the smaller nuthatch. Wedging a nut tightly in the heavily ridged bark of a nearby tree, it breaks inside with its hatchetlike bill.

The remains of securely wedged nuts are not always the work of a nuthatch. Another bird also uses the technique, seeking out suitable cracks and crevices as a natural vice to hold the nuts still while it sets to work. The greater-spotted woodpecker will also turn to a more fruitful diet when its insect food is scarce.

By night other hazelnut nibblers are at work. Both woodmice and bank voles gnaw holes in the hardening shells before clearing out the inside meal. Teeth marks around the hole are the only clue to the rodent responsible for the remains, as each dines in slightly differing ways. Even the dormouse opens the nut in an entirely individual way, leaving a clean edge and smooth rim to its intricate work.

A biting morning breeze sends the last of the autumn fall scattering and with a final flurry, the copse stands once more stripped bare. From hanging catkins to clusters of nuts, the year of the hazel is inextricably bound to the nature of the wood, the wildlife which lives amongst its branches and down amongst its roots. A constant reminder of those ancient wildwoods, the hazel copse today is still a home for birds, badgers and bright spring flowers.

Opposite: Only the male orange tip butterfly sports the flamboyant wing marking after which it is named. When folded the mottled undersides of its lower wings hide the brilliant colour and the apparent green camouflage is in fact a mix of black and yellow scales

6 LIVING WALLS

In a final fit of winter weather, a flurry of snow blows across the fields. A flock of rooks rises from the ground and flies in the face of the wind, the birds' calls mocking the so-called spring. Between the meadows a white line of icy snow marks the boundary against a steep bank surmounted by years of stifled growth. And further along, where the field joins a road, the ancient hedgerow becomes a wall of stone.

On huge predatory wings the profile of a buzzard rises rapidly into view, battling against the wind; its tail feathers fan and close, tilting from side to side as it rides the turbulent currents of air. Swept-back wings maintain constant flight without beating, and the buzzard hovers above the field. Suddenly the wings stretch out and in an instant the bird soars high into the grey leaden sky. From the air an elaborate network, measuring some thousands of miles, crisscrosses the land creating the dominant feature that is at the heart of the British country scene – a patchwork of fields divided by hedgerows and walls.

Often revealing the geology of the underlying land, walls were built for the most part of local stone; but where materials are imported from other regions, they can create islands of stone in areas of different rock strata – a feature reflected in the flora.

While stone gives a wall its strength, age gives it character; and where bare rock has weathered over the years the surface becomes more porous. Pioneer plants, the lichens, then begin to grow, thriving where the air is clean and unpolluted and combining the virtues of a photosynthetic alga with the tenacity and strength of a fungus. They are extraordinary plants, quite able to grow where no other plants have gone before, and they can survive long periods of deluge or drought. The fungus part of the alliance produces acids that etch into the rock surface, providing a secure footing. These acids also convert the rock minerals into a chemical form which the

Opposite: Weathered by wind and rain, with ivy creeping between the stones, the age of a wall can be guessed from the spread of lichen growth which add to the structure's character and colour. Though different lichen will grow at different rates, churchyard stones or other walls with dates can show the size of growth

alga can absorb. Living within that fungal framework, the alga's complex chemical reaction is fueled by minerals from the rock, and carbon dioxide and water from the air. Sunshine then fires the process and the resulting food is sustenance for both the alga and the fungus. It is a curious combination which enables the fungus to colonise new and sterile ground, for without the alga it cannot lead an independent life, whereas the alga can survive alone. Yet despite their apparent intimacy they reproduce separately – each generation forming its own new association. Together they create a large and successful group of plants, taking a variety of forms from flattened to curled and crusty.

Where lichens have led the way, mosses soon follow. Growing in the moister cracks and crevices, these compact tufts of green sport their sporophytes in spring. Raised on threadlike stalks above the rock-hugging moss, ripe brown spores are released into the wind. After years of mossy growth, a rich humus builds up on the wall between the stones – just enough soil to allow delicate-looking ferns to flourish, unfurling their pale green fronds.

Once the pioneering plants have gained a secure toehold, the seeds of annuals, drifting in the wind, land on the wall – the flowers have arrived. A miniature replay echoing botanical evolution in the colonisation of the land. Tiny spiders make the wall their world and the network of sticky threads eventually holds more than just their prey. Seeds of dandelion and herb Robert, held by webs, are washed in by the next downpour of rain. At first it is a tenuous hold but growing roots soon permeate the tiniest of cracks.

The ivy-leaved toadflax is one of the most attractive plants with a relatively recent history in Britain. Introduced from Italy and the Balkans, it has been recorded in British walls only since 1640. Shedding seeds can be a wasteful process and one which this plant seems partly to have solved. Its tiny flowers grow on elongated stalks towards the light but, as soon as pollination occurs, the growing stem turns away from the sun to seek the shelter of shade. Arching over, its newly formed seedhead grows into the nearest dark cleft. That, however, is not the only way seeds are spread along a wall. Ants will carry the seeds and even take them from wall to wall. Ants are useful creatures to flowers of the mural kind – by moving soil into cracks and carrying seeds back to their nests they facilitate the spread of plants. Many a germination owes its location to the lost cargo of a six-legged transporter.

Left to the ravages of time and weather even the strongest structures will begin to decay. Breaches soon grow if a wall is not repaired, revealing the nature of its construction – a strong outer shell of stone infilled with an assortment of soil and rubble. Variations on this mural theme have produced a range of appearances but whether mortared or dry stoned, hedgebanked or

Opposite: Red valerian is a common plant of walls well able to withstand the often harsh and dry conditions. Thick succulent leaves are a drought resistant feature and its mass of tiny flowers are a favourite with many butterflies

Standing firm an old stone wall has kept cattle and sheep secure for many years. A vantage point for birds, with cracks and crevices harbouring hundreds of smaller animals there is more to these stone structures than at first meets the eye

freestanding, a good wall will retain its strength for many years. When well built, it will be dry inside, with infill prevented from being washed away by the slab of stone that covers its top.

Another flower alien to Britain is the so-called Oxford ragwort – a plant that is thought to have literally gone over the wall, escaping from the Oxford botanic gardens. A native of Sicily, growing on Mount Etna's volcanic slopes, its preference for freedraining sites made walls a natural choice.

From the bottom of these artificial cliffs a lush growth of plants can appear; for some it is a sheltered site, with the advantage of minerals washed from the surface above; for others it is a base from which to climb – the goose grass with its hairy leaves and prickly stems that aid its upward growth. Goose grass, too, can be spread by creatures, but ones considerably larger than ants. A sheep, rubbing against the wall or just grazing at its foot, can carry away the entire prickly plant that has tangled in its coat.

Ants move in through the smallest of gaps and create sizeable cavities for the growth of the colony's black-bodied horde. Industrious little workers,

Opposite: Where mosses and lichens lead the way enough soil soon accumulates for seeds of higher plants to germinate on top of the wall. Herb robert is a familiar flower of banks and hedgerows which will also grow between stones

Slow worms will seek out the warmth of sun baked stones and so are naturally drawn to low level walls, wherever there is sufficient cover to hide. Indirect heat gained from a slate or wooden board is most often preferred

garden black ants move earth a grain at a time, eventually shifting a surprising quantity of soil. Protecting the colony from enemies, the stonewalled nest and covering of earth also improves the microclimate in which ants prefer to live.

The social life of the ant is a complex communal organisation, which forms the basis of their busy little lives. Indeed theirs is the only insect group which has no solitary species. During the winter the colony moves deep inside or under the wall, but with warmer days of spring, miniature spoil heaps, spilling from the base between the stones, reveal their renewed activity.

The deeper cracks and crevices shaded from the noonday sun are often occupied by the familiar large shells of slow-moving snails, the garden land snail being one of the most commonly seen on warm moist nights. Mornings reveal the telltale trails of slime glistening in the sun. Hibernating deep inside stone cavities in winter, snails emerge only for the summer months. Surprisingly long lived, a snail may roam the same patch for up to six years, often returning each dawn to the same place, hidden by dense vegetation. Where walls are made of limestone or the mortar carries a concentration of lime, the calcium present provides the vital shell-building elements for snails and other armoured creatures.

Of all the plants which grow or climb up walls none can be so prolific as the ivy. Along the length of its branches, excepting the oldest, grow tiny adventitious roots which are supportive rather than sustaining. These fasten the plant directly onto the stone, enabling the ivy to climb and eventually cover its support. If left, the thickening stems will prise open cracks and dislodge the stones. After decades of unrestricted growth it may well be the ivy that supports a crumbling wall. That covering, however, harbours a habitat for many forms of life, from nesting birds to hibernating insects.

Amid the ivy the pale yellow wings of a brimstone butterfly reflect the leaves' dark green hue — a near perfect camouflage for an insect which hides to survive the winter's cold and rain. With the arrival of warmer weather, a gentle breeze ruffling the ivy stirs life into sleeping wings. From within the jungle of spangled leaves a brimstone butterfly slowly awakens. Its wings shiver and progressively open, vibrating muscles generate much needed warmth. Transformed from suspended sleep to fluttering flight, the bright yellow brimstone celebrates the coming of spring.

A small brown-grey bird, sitting on an overhead wire, is alert for a possible meal. Darting up in an aerobatic loop, it deftly picks a passing fly from the air with an audible snap of its beak. Diving down, it flies straight at a wall. The spotted flycatcher is a quiet retiring bird, wintering in tropical Africa and

Small and striking, the apparently furious and fast pace of life for the ruby-tailed wasp is not without reason. Found on walls and wooden fences and wherever there are nests of solitary bees this parasitic wasp will be active

spending its summer nesting in British walls. Hidden behind a creeper, the nest, an untidy tangle of moss, wool and hair, hangs sheltered by the stone and surrounding leaves. Held together by cobwebs, the nest may be rebuilt as the birds return year after year to the same site. A pair of spotted flycatchers can rear up to five young at a time. But the bird has a rather confusing name — only the juveniles have spots, the adults are rather plain.

In contrast to the unobtrusive catcher of flies, the presence of the house sparrow is announced by its continual chatter. Wherever there are suitable holes in barn walls and buildings, the sociable sparrow will be there. Often found in small grounded gatherings, either dusting or courting a mate, the sparrow is a familiar sight and sound on farms throughout the land. Several pairs may even share the same entrance leading to their individual nests. Occupied sites are sometimes betrayed by an untidy collection of straw and grass seen hanging from the hole. And where secure sites are in short supply, sparrows will commandeer the next best thing — house martins' old nests.

Like the flycatcher, the house martin is a summer visitor nesting beneath the shelter of an overhanging eave. The mud for its nest is collected from a nearby pond or stream and glued piece by piece to the wall and roof. Some old nests will be repaired and used again by the first martins to return, while late arrivals will have to build from new.

Some thirty-two different species of European birds are known to frequent walls, whether as shelter for a roost, a place to nest or as a regular source of food. Swifts, starlings and pigeons will all nest in holes of varying size, but the bird to use one of the smallest holes is the blue tit. Squeezing through where mortar has fallen away to create a cavity inside, these bright adaptable birds build their mossy featherlined nests high up, safe and secure. Where a stone or brick has become dislodged, robins, redstarts or blackbirds will nest, but as an occupier of holes wrens will use them not just as places to nest but as regular retreats in winter. Small birds lose heat when not active in cold weather and so wrens huddle together for warmth inside a hole for the night. Up to thirty of these tiny brown birds have been seen entering one roost just as darkness falls. There are even records of a hundred or more wrens having been counted out and back.

Within the deeper cracks and wall crevices, low down away from the heat of the sun, the tiny trundling forms of woodlice shelter by day. Only at night do they emerge to scavenge for their diet of decaying vegetation. It is after dark, too, that the scraping of shells on stone sounds the emergence of snails. On a still night it is possible to hear the rasping bite of wandering snails as they eat tender young leaves along the base of the wall and the sound will even carry far beyond. Noisier still are the snuffles and grunts of foraging hedgehogs as they feed on the snails' delicate flesh. Yet while escargots of the garden snail variety are relished by some, the British human population cannot be considered to be a major predator.

Hedgehogs are not the only nocturnal nibblers of these molluscan morsels; badgers will also take large numbers during the night. Bank voles

The weasel is an active, agile, little hunter that regularly hunts through the holes and tunnels that penetrate dry stone walls in search of its rodent prey and any other possible food

and even wood mice sometimes show a particular predilection for snails; a carefully opened shell, gnawed around the whorl, is often all that remains of a bank vole's meal.

Not all walls are completely made of stone. Those of many old barns and farmhouses are composed of cob – a mixture of clay, gravel and straw raised on a stone foundation. Immensely strong, when protected from the weather, their structures last for centuries; but where the outer protecting layer has eroded away on a sunny south-facing side, tiny holes and buzzing sounds are the signs of solitary mining bees. Although leading individual lives, they can sometimes be found in large numbers. A closer look at the coarse weathered cob can reveal the partly-eroded smooth-sided cells of past generations of bees. The hairy-legged mining bee is just one of some sixty different types found in Britain, though only a few live in walls. Excavating a narrow tunnel and shuffling backwards to expel a fine shower of soil, the bee constructs individual cells that lead off the central shaft. Each cell is lined with mud then a single egg is laid.

Mining bees are not the only insects to go where tunnels are easily made and other bigger bees, such as the red-tailed bumble bee, will use the larger holes. Tiny by comparison with the bees, the beautifully striking and irridescent ruby-tail wasp has the habits of a cuckoo. Found wherever there

127

are solitary bees and wasps, it runs rapidly, tapping its antennae as it goes, searching for nesting tunnels. Entering a shaft with impunity, protected by her thick armoured skin, the female rub-tail lays an egg in one or more of the cells. When the wasp grub eventually hatches it will gorge on the emerging young bee. And in the case of solitary wasps that provide their young with a caterpillar for food, the ruby-tail grub may consume that as well.

Although mining bees basically all belong to the same family they vary in habit and form. Some emerge in July and produce a second generation in the same season, while others take an entire year to complete their life cycle. Whether they burrow in earth banks, old mortar or cob walls, mining bees lead solitary lives in surprisingly social surroundings.

In summer, as the wall dries out, a scorching sun can create conditions on top which resemble a desert. The plants that survive and even flourish in the drought are those with thick fleshy leaves — an adaptation to reduce their water loss — the yellow flowered stonecrop is an example of a plant that thrives in the heat. As stones begin to warm and shade shrinks on a midsummer morning, soaring temperatures correspond to the increasing leap of a striped little predator — the zebra spider is aptly named — and the warmer it becomes the further it can jump.

While many spiders live in a world of silken thread, continually sensing the tensions of their traps for food, others hunt by sight. The zebra spider is one of the most highly adapted hunters of the wall. A large pair of eyes to the front, with six smaller ones to the top, give this spider near all-round vision and an almost comically human appearance. When seen at close quarters it will turn and stare, gazing up with its big black eyes — an endearing trait for a spider. Spinning a lifeline wherever it goes, the zebra spider can jump with ease across gaps in the stone that are many times its size. Catching sight of potential prey as it patrols its vertical patch, it will jump with amazing speed. Any struggle is then quickly ended with a single venomous bite. When a mural chasm far too wide to jump is encountered, the zebra spider adopts a different tactic. Paying out to the wind a line of sticky thread, the spider will wait until the line has caught on the far side of the gap, demonstrating that it is not just a jumper but an agile climber as well.

There are almost as many different species of spider found on walls as there are ways of catching food. Competition is reduced by feeding, hunting and trapping at different times or by specialising in one particular prey. The velvety brown Dysdera spider has long widely spaced fangs and hunts the mural maze of nooks and crannies in search of its woodlouse quarry. Others build a funnel-shaped web deep into a hole. Threads radiating out from the entrance act as delicate tripwires, warning of the imminent approach of any possible prey. But perhaps more familiar, and certainly more easily seen, are the hammock hung webs, suspended from the wall. These exploit the less sure-footed creatures of the manmade cliff and catch insects falling from above.

The top of a wall is a useful vantage point for birds, and their droppings

RETURN TO THE WALL

All garden plants whether flowers, shrubs or trees owe their origin to the wild. Collected and nurtured in cultivation, crossed and hybridised, created new varieties, enhanced habit and form for the grower, and produced a bewildering display of different colours.

Stone walls can be as much a feature of the home and garden as lawns and carefully planted trees, adding another dimension. But for plants to survive on walls where the conditions are often extreme, requires resistance to drought and heat, and exposure to wind and frost. So for centuries plants have been taken from walls in the wild and subjected to selective breeding. The southern European and Mediterranean grown yellow wallflower and the reddish purple snapdragon, are two of the old time favourites found in cottage gardens. The red valerian is another wall dwelling flower introduced to English gardens back in the middle ages from the south. While the Mexican fleabane arrived later in the 1860s. It is a prolific flowering daisy originally brought in to the Channel Island of Guernsey. All have since escaped from garden cultivation and returned to their original home – the wall, but this time in Britain.

add to the vital nutrients needed for growing plants. Some droppings even contain seeds but few will survive the harsh parched or windswept conditions. There is one bird, however, which uses a wall as a song post to proclaim its territory as well as using it as a source of food and as a means to obtain that food. Scattered around a fallen stone, fragmented shells show the success of a song thrush's technique. A favoured stone or wall top is used to break open snail shells – it's known as an anvil.

A handsome speckle-breasted bird, the song thrush peers into likely crevices in search of suitably sized snails. Returning to the anvil with its prize, several sideways flips are needed to smash enough of the shell so that another crack on the stone will allow the mollusc to be swallowed whole. One snail is a large meal for a thrush but one that requires a good deal of time and energy, so snails tend to be eaten mainly when other food is hard to find, towards the end of winter or in late summer when the ground is hard and worms are few and far between.

Gathering dusk brings a renewal of activity to the wildlife of the wall and snails crawl from their daytime retreats. It is a time when predators can lurk almost unseen since betraying a presence would limit any chance of success. But where the prey is as slow as a snail, the speed of attack is no real surprise and even if the hunter carried a light, it would still not limit its chances. In the steadily increasing darkness ponderous little predators come in search of slow-moving prey – the larvae of glow-worms feed mainly on snails.

Strangely misnamed, the glow-worm is an insect not a worm – though, in defence of the name, the female and grub bear little resemblance to beetles, the family to which they belong. From egg to adult the glow-worm carries a cold chemical light and the female is by far the brighter. For such a delightful creature the larva has a far from delicate way of feeding. Grasping a slug or snail with its jaws, it injects digestive juices which reduce the unfortunate victim to liquid, ready for ingestion. The patchy distribution of these illuminating insects is reflected by the presence of the prey. Snails are generally restricted to areas of limestone and chalk, but walls containing lime can also extend their range.

129

The common lizard is a frequent reptilian wall dweller hunting across the face and in between the stones. The sunlit side is where they can be found, basking in the morning to warm themselves, after the cool of the night

On a midsummer's night, beneath a celestial canopy of twinkling light, evening dew dampens the grass. Ideal conditions for amphibians to roam from their daytime hiding places – ground-level gaps between the stones. At night toads actively search for food, turning their attention to any likely prey. Striking at lightning speed with an extensible tongue they swallow, literally, in the blink of an eye. Their bulbous sockets retracting downwards into the roof of the mouth forces food into the gullet.

Frogs, too, sheltering by day will hunt along the base of the wall by night, returning to the safety of a damp crevice at dawn. A distant faint glow on the far horizon signals the coming of day. After a clear cool night, stones warm to a rising sun and the nocturnal life of the wall hides away.

The sounds of summer vibrate as grasshoppers and crickets climb for a vantage point, broadcasting their stridulant calls. Reflecting the warmth of the season, lizards bask in the sun. When they first emerge in the morning, they flatten their reptilian bodies to absorb maximum heat, as they become active only when warm. Sensing the air with a flick of their forked tongues, they move off in search of insects and spiders.

The common lizard is a wary, watchful reptile when warmed, but sluggish and shy when cold. Its long tapering tail can be nearly twice the length of its body and is an asset that lizards can afford to lose; if grabbed by a predator a violent muscle contraction will sever the tail from its owner. A remarkable device to confuse an attacker, this is achieved by a plane of weakness across a tail bone. In an almost mesmeric way, the independent wriggling and twitching tail continues its macabre dance, diverting attention while the lizard makes good its narrow escape. Many predators will then consume the discarded lure. Later, regeneration of the healed stump forms a brand new tail and, although not as long or thin, it retains much of the same character as the old, albeit with a simpler covering of scales.

Perhaps as a response to the cooler climate of northern Europe, the female of the common lizard does not risk the uncertainty of egg laying but retains her young inside. In late summer she gives birth to fully formed baby lizards, encased in a protective egg sac. The sac is then either ruptured at birth, or soon after, by the hatchling's snout. The first few weeks of life are precarious for the young – eaten by birds, frogs and toads, even their own kind are not averse to taking tiny lizards.

The quick-moving common lizard is not alone when it comes to wall-frequenting reptiles. The slow-worm, despite its snakelike appearance and deceptive name, is a legless lizard. Flat loose stones on top of a low wall are a favoured hiding place. And as to how the reptile climbs, its name belies its sudden turns of speed and the way it can crawl up between the crevices. Not

Deep within the wall a hollow cavity is home to a colony of wasps. But by the end of summer only newly emerged queens are left to carry the seeds of a new working brood into the following year

ONCE UPON A WALL

The broad turf topped stone wall stretching away from the road looked from the car to be an interesting site, surrounded by fields and woods. The sloe fruits of late summer and the beginning of the blackberry crop hung down over its edge. A lizard slipped along between its granite boulders and wasps were working hard, carrying back their captured prey in a flying fleet of striped bodies. Alighting on the stone runway they disappeared into the dark. Shrubs sprawled its length but where there were gaps the sun scorched stems of grass swayed in the breeze. The sound of grasshoppers and lazily buzzing bees cut through the distant noise of the traffic. A wren searched from where pennywort sprung between weathered grey stones, and lichens grew in the sun. But down in the damp and shade only mats of moss could be found, except where soil spilled from the hole of an excavating mouse.

As the season matured so did the fruit and the insect life died away, but with each time of passing the sight of that wall reminded me of that warm summer's day until the developers board went up. Now that wall lie at the bottom of someone's garden.

as fast as the common lizard, the slow-worm seldom basks in the open. An attack from a passing predator can come from land or air. Overhead, in hovering silhouette, a kestrel regularly patrols the farm walls. From high above the bird descends, a step at a time, on sighting an eye-catching movement. A sudden stoop on folding wings and a lizard becomes another link in the food chain of the farm.

The growth of much of the mural flora slows or comes to an end with the ripening of fruit. Blackberries, large and luscious, hang invitingly off the wall – perhaps a night-time meal for a visiting bank vole. Huge clusters of thick-leaved, red valerian flowers stand out in a still blue sky, butterflies – meadow brown and gatekeeper, peacock and tortoiseshell – feed from its tiny blooms.

A wall brown butterfly basks where it ought, before resuming its territorial flight. There are times when the air seems to be buzzing with insect life and other times when all seems strangely quiet. Not so obvious, but surprisingly common late in the year, a tiny black and red wasp runs frantically, searching over the wall. Investigating every nook and cranny, under leaves and stones the spider-hunting wasp seeks out its eight legged prey. A spider as large as the wasp is paralysed by its sting, but is still not dead. Dragged back along the wall, it is pulled up stone faces, along ledges and through the vegetation. The wasp always runs the risk of being taken by an even larger spider while dragging its prey. Eventually returning to its burrow, the female wasp lays her egg within her victim's body – a crude but effective way of supplying the young with fresh food on hatching.

More obvious than the solitary wanderings of one little wasp are the comings and goings of the social kind. A small entrance hole conceals a cavity filled by a large ball of a nest begun the previous spring. A single queen wasp, mated the year before, emerged from her winter hibernation to build the beginnings of the nest literally from scratch. Using her powerful jaws she scraped off shavings of wood from convenient trees and fence posts. Chewed and mixed with saliva, the pulp was moulded into a wasp-sized ball which she carried back to the chosen site. The nest is made up from layer upon layer of paper. Containing tiers of galleried cells, in the short space of summer it grew steadily as more workers took over the initial work. Supported by its own strength the lightweight structure has now become a nursery and home for some twenty thousand insects.

Honey bees will also utilise the safety of a hole in the wall, producing their hanging combs of wax laden with honey. Untouched and undisturbed by natural predators or beekeepers alike, these near natural hives can grow to a substantial size but only if room permits.

Towards the end of summer the area around the bee colony can take on the appearance of a battlefield; the bodies of dead wasps littering the ground reveal little of the drama inside. As the year comes to an end for a nearby colony of wasps the workers, released from their daily chores, are joined by drones in their seasonal craving for sweetness. And it is now that the wasps become a nuisance to man and to bees. Attempting to steal from the heavy honey-filled combs the wasps are met by the defending bees. In a bid to protect their winter stores the bees, at this time of the year, are at their most defensive. It is a battle the wasps are bound to lose, vastly outnumbered as they are by bees. Sacrificing their lives for the colony, the honey bees attack and attempt to sting the invading wasps to death. Locked in mortal combat they fall to the floor. The dead and dying bodies of both wasps and bees are then unceremoniously dumped outside by the honey-gathering workers. It is

Not such a prickly life as it first appears these hedgehogs, though only a few days old and with needle sharp spines, remain unharmed. It's only when disturbed that the spines stand erect and become an impaling defence

an annual conflict that ends only when the wasps are killed off by the first frosts of autumn.

In a final show of muted colour the ivy is the last to flower. Its pollen and nectar give a final boost to the winter stores of bees and vital sustenance for butterflies before they, too, settle into hibernation. An entire wild community lives alongside and also within a structure built by man. For some, it is the centre of their short lives, for others, it may be the venue only of a flying visit. For that wildlife, walls are much more than just stone.

A sparrowhawk circles in a patchy cloud-filled sky, scanning the countryside below. Seen from the air, walls make up only a small proportion of the land's dividing assets; by far the greatest is the hedgerow. A vast irregular lattice spanning valleys and surrounding moors, the hedge is more than a boundary to a field.

The autumn hedge boasts its ripening berries in a landscape subdued by a dampness that hangs heavily in the air. A light morning mist and a cool start to the day mark the end of the year. Ploughed fields, and the distant roar of a tractor cutting its broad swathe of dark-brown earth, are seasonal features of the farm.

The hedgerow is a mass of warm faded colour. The dry twisted leaves begin to drop. Down where the margin of the field meets this ancient living border, the rustling of prickles and leaves is not an uncommon sound. A hedgehog foraging by day in autumn is a familiar country sight. Increasing its fat reserves for a winter sleep takes more time than there are hours in the night. The hedgehog holds a special place in the hearts of town and country dwellers. Yet few people know much about its mainly nocturnal habits, few can separate fact from the fiction of myth. Feeding largely on caterpillars, earthworms, slugs and snails, beetles and even the occasional bird's egg, this prickly mammal forages widely in search of food. Stopping frequently to sniff the air, its eyesight is poor when compared to its acute reaction to sound and smell. Hedgehogs are remarkably noisy animals for their size, snuffling and snorting especially when courting a mate.

An increasing supply of food is required as the days progressively shorten. Dropping temperatures signal the start of the winter hibernation. Retreating to a nest of leaves and grass under the cover of a bush or inside a convenient hole, the hedgehog prepares for a long deep sleep, so profound that it is difficult to be certain if the animal is still alive. Curling up, head tucked into its belly, the paws and eyes are tightly closed. Its body temperature slowly falls to only a few degrees from death. Just above freezing the muscles set rigid and breathing slows to an irregular ten breaths a minute. The heart rate slows dramatically, one beat every three seconds – a tenth of its normal level. The animal is barely alive. Surviving on layers of brown and white fat converted from its autumn food, with the kidney function almost ceasing so as to conserve water, unseen physiological changes allow the body to survive. The composition of the hedgehog's blood changes as white corpuscles leave to surround the digestive system, guarding against bacterial

Red admiral butterflies are one of the last to be seen on the wing on warmer days even into winter. The autumn flowering ivy then becomes a vital source of sustenance for many other insects as well

infection developing in the gut. Amazingly, even in this state of suspended animation, a sudden noise will cause prickles to be raised, though it would still take many hours to raise the animal fully from its sleep.

Despite the incredible complexity of seasonal survival technique, it is not entirely infallible. The first year is the most critical for, if the young hedgehog fails to lay down sufficient fat, it may die during hibernation. Probably fewer than one in three survive their first winter, though in subsequent years their chances are very much higher.

Spring sees the emergence of a thinner streamlined hedgehog. Gone is the rotund prickly ball filled with accumulated fat; the urgency now is to feed and then breed. A safe nest is made by the female, sometimes inside a wall or down a deserted burrow, ready to receive her brood. Young hedgehogs are born pink, helpless and blind, no different to many of their kind, but the presence of prickles soon sets them apart from other small mammals. Within an hour of birth sharp white prickles push through the skin on their backs. This is then followed in a day and a half by a second wave of darker brown spines, between the first. When it comes to noise, the young hedgehogs seem to start in the way they mean to go on, at first making a high-pitched piping sound, reminiscent of baby birds.

A nest of hedgehogs would appear to be a rather inhospitable place. But

SLAVE LABOUR

A tiny industrious army can be found camping beneath many stone walls, exploring and plundering the surrounding country for food and vital supplies. Ants live in a remarkably well organised community that centres on the nest and queen, with the various chores of its society destined from birth. The colonies are remarkably long-lived, lasting for many years and while workers may come and go in a season the queen can survive much longer. The raising of new queens then ensures the survival of the colony.

The lives of some species can be as complex as the nest structure, with cases of social parasitism and slavery not at all uncommon. A mated queen will seek out the nest of a closely related ant and once accepted will then lay her own eggs. Eventually she and her kind take over the running of the colony. Even more incredible is the way workers of the red sanguinea ant raid another species nest to carry off pupae as potential slaves. The queen of the raiding army first produces some ants that set off to capture a new brood of slaves before constructing a home. The newly hatched slaves then work to establish the sanguinea colony.

surprisingly their spines, when not erect, can be almost as soft as hair. There are generally between three and five hedgehogs to a litter, and with eyes opening within two weeks they begin to leave the nest after a further ten days. The first foraging trips are usually made in the company of an adult. Learning to find their own food on these family forays eventually leads to an independent life.

One of the most curious sides of a hedgehog's conduct is the process of self-annointing. Working its saliva into a froth it spreads it liberally over its spines with a surprising degree of energetic contortion. Whether to strengthen or to mask its scent is not fully understood but whatever the purpose it remains a tangible if mysterious part of the hedgehog's nocturnal behaviour.

The hedgerow is an avenue of life linking woodlands large and small. Typically a tangle of many different shrubs, the variety and richness of farmland wildlife owes not a little to the hedge. Perhaps therefore surprisingly, only one butterfly caterpillar is confined almost exclusively to a hedgerow bush. The brimstone larvae eat buckthorn leaves, though many other larvae feed in the herb layer down below. Wall brown and gatekeepers feast on grass, while peacock and small tortoiseshell caterpillars consume the fresh growth of nettles. Even garlic mustard, more appropriately known as jack-by-the-hedge, is eaten by the caterpillars of orange tip and green-veined white.

The bright eye-catching wings of butterflies make them the most obvious insects by day. But after dark a host of nocturnal fliers lay their eggs in hedgerow trees. More than a hundred different moth caterpillars are known to feed on hawthorn and nearly as many again on blackthorn – a population which reflects the ancient origin of these common hedgerow shrubs.

There is nothing quite like an early summer hedge in full bloom; a blaze of

Opposite: The even slope of a newly faced Devon walled-bank is almost a work of art, with rounded stones set side by side and topped with lines of turf. The many variations on the mural theme merely reflecting the availability of stone as well as local tradition

colour and humming with life. Fresh green growth, beginning to spread from its close-cropped lines, covers the movements of small mammals – shrews and voles. Another movement suddenly catches the eye and the figure of a standing stoat peers above the grass. Bobbing down and up again to see if the human intruder has gone, stoats are immensely curious. If one remains quite still the animal will often approach, its black-tipped tail and larger size distinguishing it from a weasel.

Along the hedgerows, walls and buildings, the stoat's main quarry is the rabbit, but it also hunts voles, birds and mice. Relentlessly pursuing its principal prey in and out, down and around a maze of burrowed tunnels, the stoat will even chase a chosen victim through a whole colony of rabbits, which amazingly continue to graze, apparently unaware of the running drama with a fatal end. By contrast the sight of a stoat family, frolicking and playing amongst a pile of fallen rocks, is a fascinating spectacle to behold. Seen from a distance the animals can appear as a sinuous brown line, diving in and out the tumbled tunnels and bridges of stone.

If the summer hedge bulges with verdant life then the growing tinge of autumn colours are highlighted by scarlet and shining black fruit – rosehips, honeysuckle and blackberries ripening in the sun. Between hedge base and the open field wind-beaten corn, which escaped the combine's rotating steel clutches, lies on the ground. And along with wild fruit and seeds, it provides a feast for a foraging flock of finches – a colourful group of mixed gold and green – chaffinches and red-tinted linnets. Even sparrows join the twittering party for this brief annual harvest.

Apart from finches other small birds exploit the comparative safety and advantages of feeding in flocks; a mixed group of titmice, blue and great as well as longtailed, join to forage the woodlands and the hedgerow trees. Hopping from pillar to post, from branches to stems, they feed on the remaining caterpillars which have yet to pupate.

Noisy gatherings are always likely to attract attention and the hit-and-run tactician of the bird world – the sparrowhawk – seizes its chance. Breaking away from its woodland patrol, this master of surprise streaks in towards the chattering flocks. Brief glimpses of its speeding shape on the far side of the hedge are the only signs that betray its deadly intentions. A sudden jink through a seemingly impassable gap and the sparrowhawk plucks a blue tit from the air, a few floating yellow feathers mark its demise. Almost before the other birds have time to react the hawk has gone up, over and beyond the hedge in a smooth aerial roll. Scattered by the sudden encounter, the flock regain their respective excitedly chattering groups before continuing to glean their seasonal feed.

The hedgerow has a natural importance out of all proportion to its manmade needs and as such is far more than an earth bank topped with trees and covered with growing weeds.

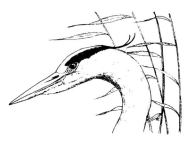

7 THE POND

On the first mild night of the New Year the grass is soaking wet. For the past few weeks sleet and snow from the east have alternated with cold dry days, but a warm weather front moving in from across the Atlantic Ocean, with moist south-westerly winds, signals the start of the annual amphibian gathering first in Devon and Cornwall. During the weeks that follow, on warm wet nights, across the country millions of migrating frogs head for their spawning grounds. A hopping horde piles into several small ponds as though they were the only suitable fresh water for miles around – a fact sometimes not so far from the truth.

Ponds were once far more than just a feature to be found on farmland since they played an essential part in maintaining the livestock of the farm. Today the traditional pond is no longer needed as a source of fresh water and many have been filled in or drained. But when left undisturbed and unpolluted, the old farm pond can become a wild oasis on a well kept farm. Where cattle once trampled the edge and stirred its muddy depths plants now grow tall around its margins.

Many frogs will have overwintered in the mud of a pond, while others begin to congregate from wintering sites across miles of surrounding meadows. The males are the first to arrive, drawn by the almost imperceptible smell of an alga – a growth which will provide the tadpoles with their first food. In the shallows, warmed by a weak winter sun, the nightly croaking chorus attracts the female frogs. At first glance, all frogs may appear the same, but in contrast to the slippery skinned males, the females have lines of tactile granulations running down their backs, as well as being heavily distended.

In the water some male frogs grab at any thing that moves. Other males struggle and kick, uttering a distinctive grunt, while females swollen with spawn each submit to the clasp of a male. Special pads on the male's thumbs enable him to hold onto his mate until the eggs are released – perhaps after several hours.

It is an extraordinary mêlée and if seen from underwater a new dimension is added to the sight. Below the surface, in subdued aquatic sound and slow swimming motion, a female frog is held in an amorous embrace. Pressing her front feet against her own belly to assist with the laying, she suddenly produces a continuous stream of spawn. Fertilised at the same time, up to

3,000 black eggs are laid in just a few seconds. The frogs soon part, leaving the spawn to sink and swell. Because the individual gelatinous coats then absorb water, the eggs become buoyant and float to the surface. Within twenty-four hours the spawn has reached its maximum, familiar size. A soft transparent gel protects the developing tadpole, not just from predators unable to consume the jellylike mass, but more importantly, it acts as an insulating layer, maintaining the spawn's temperature up to two degrees above that of the surrounding water.

Clearing clouds reveal the darkness of the sky lit only by a celestial arc of stars and, as the insulating cloud layer passes, the air temperature drops by the hour. At dawn an early morning sun rises on a frosted scene. Winter has still to release its icy grip and the pond has frozen once more. Beneath the ice some movement can still be seen. A pair of frogs, still in a cold embrace, move in near-frozen slow motion, able to survive under the ice where the water is a few degrees warmer. Near the surface the picture is different. Growing fingers of ice have killed the upper layers of spawn. Even in death the jelly still adds to the insulation of the eggs below – so some will survive. A severe spell of intense cold could completely freeze the shallows and any early laid spawn would be killed along with any adults trapped in the advancing ice. One advantage of Britain's notoriously fickle climate is that extremes of cold seldom stay for long and within a day or so a thaw will have brought renewed activity to the pond.

Over the following days and nights the wet weather continues to see more bulging female frogs arrive, crawling and hopping from the surrounding grass. Hundreds, and even thousands of frogs may be attracted to one pond alone. And if the weather stays fair for the few days of spawning, they will disappear almost as quickly as they came.

Croaking amphibian gatherings are conspicuous early in the year; a time when little other food is available and predators can take a heavy toll. The heron is a frequent year-round visitor for, at any time, one or two frogs may be found; but the annual spawning provides an opportunity not to be missed. Landing a little way from the edge of the pond, a heron walks into the water. Craning its long neck straight, it peers intently down its daggerlike beak,

A FROZEN ASSET

The life of a pond in winter survives because water is unique. A layer of ice forms first on top while the water below remains above freezing. In all other liquids increasing cold causes it to become more dense and eventually turn to solid. The remarkable property of water is that it steadily shrinks as its density increases until it reaches four degrees centigrade. It then begins to expand as the temperature continues to drop, and as ice is less dense than the surrounding water, it floats to the top. The thicker the frozen layer the better the insulation but once water has turned to ice its temperature can continue to drop, so any creature caught in its grip will freeze solid.

Life below remains active, though the cold keeps it sluggish, and near frozen fish and slow moving frogs make catching a meal for a mink or a heron, that much easier. Standing at the pondside the patience of one particular heron was stretched for more than an hour. The frogs, hardly moving, lay just below the surface but between bird and breakfast lay a thick window of ice.

Clasped in an amorous embrace a pair of frogs are ready to produce their spawn in shallow water at the edge of the pond. Perhaps the same stretch of water in which they swam as tadpoles a few years before

waiting motionless in an apparently awkward stance. A breeze ruffling its long black-feathered crest is the only sign of movement, then, without warning, it strikes and catches a frog; a flick of the head and the frog is swallowed whole. A few steps tentatively forward and the whole process is repeated again and again. Despite the preoccupation of the coupling frogs, they are still no easy prey. With their bodies submerged but eyes still above water, they are sensitive to the slightest move and quickly duck out of sight.

Also arriving by air, another avian hunter seems to show a strange seasonal preference for hunting at ponds. From a nearby vantage point a buzzard, sitting on a branch, waits for any amphibian landing. It is when entering or leaving the water that frogs are most at risk. A quick flap of the buzzard's wings and a short glide is all that is needed to grasp its slippery prey. Even at night frogs are still not safe, for although herons and buzzards do not generally hunt after dark owls most certainly do. The tawny owl will take frogs at any time of the year, but especially in spring when frog movements are more conspicuous.

A light shifting mist gently moving over the surface of the pond greets the morning sun, and ever-increasing rippled circles emanate from a quietly paddling coot. The last frost lingered briefly only two weeks before but now the warmer spring days have woken more life. The toads begin to appear.

Lying in deeper water they are more faithful to a particular pond than the earlier spawning frogs, which will change pools from year to year. Toads nearly always return to the pond of their birth, and their spawning is more in keeping with their general pace of life – a slow crawl.

The larger female is held in a clasping embrace by her mate and may take many hours to lay her eggs. Moving amongst the weed, she leaves a long trailing string of black beaded spawn while the male toad fends off other suitors with his large back feet. Composed of up to two and a half thousand eggs the fertilised necklace lies entangled in the weeds across the bottom and up the sides of the pond.

This slow-moving underwater scene is not always the way events begin. As with the frogs, the male toads tend to arrive first, waiting for the females and uttering their funny little croaks. But when males vastly outnumber the available mates, a writhing ball of attentive toads soon envelops the most recent female arrival. A mass of toad bodies and legs rolls around in the weeds until at last a clutching pair manages to break free. Swimming with powerful back-kicking strokes, the female with her smaller attached male flees the squirming crowd.

At the end of a warm winter's day the sun is low on the western horizon, bathing the pool in a blaze of gold. A light wind rustles wintered brown leaves and the imposing pokers of majestic reedmace release their feathered seeds to be borne away on the wind. Some do not drift far before being caught by the overhanging branches of a willow, while others skim and tumble across the smooth surface of the water.

The beginning of a new day finds the downwind shore lapped by a surf of fine seed. Wading knee deep, a fox sniffs at a floating feather and stares alert across the pond. A few laps of water and with its ears twitching, turning and straining for any strange sound, the animal climbs back out onto the bank. A vigorous shake produces a fine shower, and nose down it investigates the pond's edge. Even foxes will take a frog or two if given the chance. A slight movement ahead, and the plop of a frog entering water reveals the amphibian's agility which relies on a jump to escape. The defence of the toad, however, is more subtle and lies skin deep – the toad is not as defenceless as it looks. With a quick pounce, the fox snaps at the toad and picks it up in its mouth, only to drop it almost as quickly again. Shaking its head, salivating and almost retching, the fox's distaste for the toad is apparent as it tries to relieve the unflavoursome effects. Toads are protected by powerful toxic secretions produced from their backs, and any predator that has tasted a toad will no doubt avoid the creatures in the future.

Not all predators are put off by the apparently vile taste. Hedgehogs will eat toads without any obvious signs of ill effects, while buzzards tend to

Opposite: Freshwater is as vital to wild animals as it is to domestic farm life, though the fox will also frequent the margin in search of a meal, whether amphibian or fowl and may even lie up in the surrounding reeds

remove the skin first. Even grass snakes show a marked degree of personal preference for toads – some regularly take them, others ignore them completely.

An obnoxious taste is a tried and tested defence, and one not just confined to the toad. The largest of our three native newts is the great crested or warty skinned type, which also relies on its own nauseousness as protection. The male is large and dark, and during the breeding season develops a spectacular crest along the back and tail. Underneath glowing colour covers its belly in a pattern of bold bright orange.

The males of both palmate and smooth newts, the other two species, also develop an attractive undercolour in the spring. Though differing in size and some habits, all three newts display similar seasonal features. Theirs is an elaborate aquatic courtship in which the male takes an active role and the female a passive part. The male performs a delicate ritual dance, parading his fine colours in front of the female, before fanning her with his curled tail. Releasing a scent, the vibrating, shimmering tail wafts an erotic current towards the male's chosen mate. The fan dance of the male begins with a whip of his entire body and a wave which passes from amphibian head to the tip of his quivering tail.

Eventually the female follows his lead and he deposits a tiny white packet of sperm. The female then picks up the spermatophore in her vent; the released contents fertilise the eggs and the female can begin to lay. Carefully she places a single egg at a time on an aquatic weed; each egg is protected inside a folded leaf. When spawning is complete, the newts leave the water and spend the summer amongst damp vegetation, and in winter hibernate beneath logs and stones.

Shallow ponds can suffer most of the extremes found on Earth, from flood to drought, heat and frozen cold. The fresh water that is vital to so many forms of life can offer a variety of different species many places to live. On surface skin, or in murky depth, along the margins or above the water, the life of the pond is sometimes surprisingly short lived. The shallowness of a pool can limit some species such as fish, which are unable to survive recurring droughts, and yet encourage other species, since there are fewer aquatic predators in such unpredictable ponds – amphibians spend only part of their lives in water, as do many insects.

One of the most fascinating aspects of the pond is the strength of the surface and the life on it. Water molecules are strongly attracted to each other, and with their forces concentrated at the surface alongside and below, the powerful bonds form a face to the air – a layer sufficiently strong to support the plants and small insects that exploit the extraordinary properties of this elastic skin. Relying on surface tension to bear their tiny weights,

Previous page: Far from the daily bustle of busy farm life the old pond quietly lives out its remaining years, reflecting the recent growth of aquatic vegetation. No longer needed for cattle or sheep and left alone, it has become an oasis for freshwater life

The great-crested or warty newt is today one of the rarest amphibians likely to be found in farm ponds. But it is only the male that develops the characteristic crest

some insects use water-repelling oils or wax to enable them not to break through the surface. Standing on widely splayed legs, a pond skater is supported by a thin waxy coat. But a home for one can be a lethal trap for another, and any ill equipped insect falling into the water is held by the very same forces that keep the skaters afloat. The struggling of an insect causes minute vibrations to ripple across the surface and, detecting the movement with its sensitive front legs, the water-walking predator skates in for the kill. By lifting its victim clear of the surface, the pond skater eliminates any more ripples and ensures an undisturbed meal for one.

Pond skaters are often one of the first surface dwellers to arrive on newly formed ponds, flying in from nearby ponds. Adapted for life as a water walker, the pond skater even attracts a mate by purposely vibrating the surface. The use of that surface tension to send and receive rippled signals is also exploited by the crazy gyrations of the whirlygig beetle. Reading the returning ripples like a surface-confined sonar, these beetles detect the presence in their immediate world of any intruders that enter.

The life that depends on a skin of molecular strength is remarkably varied – floating leaves, surface-running spiders and even air-breathing subaquatic insects with a wax coated tube to the air rely on this property of water, and by this means the nymphs of diving beetles and adult water scorpions

147

maintain regular links with the world above.

The ability to breathe air and yet survive under water has seen some incredible adaptations. Of the 40,000 different species of spider known in the world, only one is truly aquatic and really lives up to its name. The water spider is unique amongst its arachnid relatives, spending its entire life below surface. From birth to death, it feeds, breeds, moults and mates without ever leaving the water – yet it still needs air to breathe.

Covered in velvety hair that traps a life-giving layer, the water spider's body is cocooned in a silvery coat. Spinning its silken home down amongst the weeds and furnishing it with a bubble of air, the spider crawls to the surface only to renew a stale supply. Head down, it raises its glistening abdomen to trap a fresh bubble before returning to its diving bell. When the oxygen has been used the spider will release the old atmosphere and collect a fresh supply on several surface-running trips. But this procedure is not carried out as often as might be expected. Some carbon dioxide breathed out by the spider dissolves into the water, while a small quantity of oxygen diffuses back into the bubble, a near self-supporting function that only at times needs a hand, or rather eight legs, to renew the air.

Pond water is a rich soup of microscopic life that forms the basis for a freshwater food chain. From algal growth to the predatory heron, a host of organisms is primarily dependent on the energy of the sun – the power for the plant world's photosynthetic system. Released as a botanical byproduct, oxygen is an essential element for animal life, whether in air or under water. In the filtered shafts of dappled sunlight penetrating down from the surface, the only signs of plant activity are the tiny streams of life-supporting bubbles, emanating from every green tissue.

One of the most commonly encountered tiny crustaceans to be found in a jar of pond water is the delightfully named *Daphnia* or water flea. Floating in their millions in mid-water they filter out algae and bacteria with their legs, before passing this primary food to their mouths. What the water flea loses in size it more than makes up for in sheer numbers and, as such, is of major importance in some ponds as food for larger animals, trapped in the stinging tentacles of a delicate little hydra or snapped up by hungry fish. Yet one of the strangest crustacean consumers is not an animal but a predatory plant – the bladderwort is an insectivorous free-floating weed.

The plant bears tiny bladders which each have an opening in one end surrounded by equally small stiff bristles. The aperture is closed by a flap, forming an inward opening door, and the sensitive hairs create a funnel leading to the trap. The water fleas are apparently attracted by a mucous-producing gland near the door and on swimming in they touch a trigger hair. The response is instantaneous; the trapdoor opens and water rushes in, flea

Opposite: Upside down in an underwater world this spider is very much at home. Encased in a glistening layer of air the aquatic spider moves along the weeds in search of prey, but never far from its silken diving bell retreat

and all. The closing door then seals the flea's eventual fate. The dead and decomposing body is finally digested by the bladder's internal lining of glandular hairs, and the nutritious mix is eventually absorbed by the plant. Only in summer with the emergence of a yellow flowering spike does the greater bladderwort mark its position in the pond as a deadly *Daphnia* trap.

Dawn brings sunbathed warmth to cool water and the early morning light reveals the growth of spring – emergent plants, floating weeds and a reedbed forest beyond. Close to the mudlined bank and overhanging leaves, a black wriggling mass feeds in the shallows. Tadpoles sometimes gather in vast shoals around the warmest parts of the pond, but soon disperse if disturbed and head for deeper water. Birds are probably their greatest enemies but others are less easily seen.

Slipping quietly through the tangled fringe, a tiny grass snake hunts for a meal. Hatched at the end of last summer, it has spent the winter for the most part asleep. Now in spring its appetite draws it to the damper parts of the farm, to the pond and possible prey. More than a capable swimmer and quite at home in the water, the young snake must keep to cover, as it may well be mistaken by a bird for a worm – at this age grass snakes are little larger than pencils.

Early in the year tadpoles form an important element in the diet of a young grass snake. With comparatively large eyes and a distinct yellow collar, its olive coloured skin forms a background to the features of this reptile. Raising its tiny blunt-nosed head it peers at a wriggly movement in the water; a lunge, and a tadpole is held firm. Even young snakes can dislocate their jaws, enabling them to swallow their prey whole; the process can take more than a minute.

Hidden between the tall stems of the marginal jungle, many birds build their nests. One of the shyest is the dabchick, otherwise known as the little grebe, the smallest member of its family to nest in Europe. The nest is a floating platform of weeds anchored by other plant growth. Both the male and female share the incubation of up to six white eggs, taking turns to brood or feed – diving for sticklebacks, shrimps or water-dwelling insects. Even when not well hidden the nest is not obvious, for, despite its large size the eggs are rarely seen. When disturbed, or while feeding, an adult will cover its clutch by pulling plant material over the nest, leaving a wet rotted pile. Camouflage complete, the bird then quietly dives under water and leaves unseen.

Ungainly on land, the little grebe rarely leaves the pond, so well adapted is it to its watery world, and the chicks when only just hatched are able to swim. In response to an adult's alarm call, the young do not head back to the nest but make for a parent, to clamber out onto its back. These birds are

Opposite: The little grebe is also known as the dabchick and builds a floating platform of vegetation on which to brood their clutch, well hidden amongst the reeds out in deeper water. A shy bird that will dive away rather than risk being seen

widely distributed and are found generally on larger pools where there will often be only one pair. Differing from the shy and retiring grebe, the moorhen is noisy and aggressive, defending a territory with spectacular fights above the water. Its feet are its weapons of war and some territorial disputes can end with broken toes or dislocated thighs. Resting every so often, locked in foot-to-foot combat, the moorhens' outstretched wings balance a fighting pair. Females will also join in the fray, defending together with their mates their claim to an area of the pond.

Just as aggressive is the slightly larger coot which will also stand, or rather float, and fight, though a threat more often ends in a water-spattering pursuit. The territorial dispute usually begins with a head down, tail-and-wing-raised threat. The defender will challenge an intruder be it another coot, as well as moorhens and ducks. The coot prefers a larger expanse of water than the mud-paddling moorhen, but where ranges overlap the peace is often just an uneasy truce.

While the coot will build a substantial nest of reeds in shallow water, either floating or fixed to a fallen, partly submerged branch, the moorhen makes a smaller platform. It is a nest which is usually found close to the pond but it can sometimes be built quite high in a tree. And with the chicks of both coots and moorhens leaving the nest within two or three days of hatching, young moorhens may have to begin *their* life with a leap.

Although waterbird fledglings are vulnerable at first whilst swimming on open water, or following their parents on land, by far the greatest predation appears to be that of the eggs. There may be several brood nests scattered around the pond, which are used only as temporary or nightly retreats. Where built in deep water, a ramp of dead vegetation built alongside forms an easy access for the chicks without breaking the edge of the nest. Both moorhen and coot feed on similar foods but, while the moorhen can apparently thrive in little more than a puddle, the coot needs open water to dive for its wide variety of meals – roots and shoots of waterweeds, insects, small fish and tadpoles.

Around the pond perimeter the growth of reeds and sedge forms an effective screen for the smaller nests of buntings and for the cradle cup of the warbler. The reed bunting is not just restricted to the water's edge and in recent years it has expanded its range well away from lakes and ponds. More faithful to its name the reed warbler is found almost exclusively in reed beds, sidling up and down the stems and restlessly hopping from one to another.

Out on the water a mallard, one of the best known wild birds of farm ponds, is surrounded by a dabbling throng of ducklings. Unlike moorhens and coots it is only the duck that incubates and then tends her brood; the drake plays little or no part in the family life.

Opposite: Hidden amongst the reeds the coot usually constructs a pile of vegetation as a bird-built island to support its brood. In deeper water they may build a raft or even above the surface on a fallen branch or broken stems

With no rainfall for the past few weeks the importance of pools grows for the wildlife of the farm. Birds come, not only to drink, but for a dip, which is an essential part of their daily routine. The bright colours of a bathing yellowhammer make the bird stand out amongst a flock of spray-making sparrows energetically indulging in their bath. Feathers must be kept clean or their efficiency for flight and insulation would become impaired. Sitting in the shallows, feathers all fluffed, the birds flap their wings, spread their tails and raise their crests. Yet despite the vigour of their indulgence, it is more of a shower than a soaking, since a wet and bedraggled bird would be easy prey while unable to fly.

Early summer also sees other visitors to the pond and its surrounds, but they do not come necessarily for water. The house martin which normally keeps to the air makes a seasonal series of visits to the ground as it collects beakfuls of mud to build its plastered nest beneath the farmhouse eaves.

As they come down to drink birds are alert and wary, often using an island perch as a safer place than the bank. One bird that has overcome the need to land in order to quench its thirst is the swallow, which demonstrates its aerial expertise as it drinks while skimming the surface. Honey bees, too, make regular trips from their hives. Landing near the water's edge they imbibe considerable quantities of water for their size; mixed with honey, it becomes a beverage for larval bees.

Insects are an essential ingredient of the pond community both above and below water; for some, a few short weeks, for others, years of growth. The early stages of a dragonfly's development can take up to two years before it emerges as an adult. It begins as a carnivorous nymph, living on the bottom or hiding amongst vegetation, literally seizing its prey with an extendible mask, held beneath its head, and relying for camouflage on its colour of muddy grey, green or brown. A tadpole wriggles near but just out of reach, so the nymph begins a slow, stealthy stalk. In a flash the tadpole is caught, impaled on terminal hooks and is drawn back to the lair to be devoured. Waiting for hour after hour, these nymphs will watch, their large eyes seldom missing any movement and few small creatures are safe from their voracious grasping hunger.

After a series of moults and new growth the nymph of an emperor dragonfly is fully mature. In some species there are as few as nine sheddings while in others up to sixteen, although the average number of skin moultings is more usually twelve. When ready to emerge as a free flying adult, the nymph will rest half out of the water. Then, under cover of approaching darkness, it laboriously climbs a stem until well clear of the surface. Tiny claws dig into the plant tissue and the nymph securely embraces the stem. It is a life or death hold as its grip must support the emerged adult which will

Opposite: The reed warbler true to name builds a cup shape nest supported waist high by reeds. Yet its habit is not always exclusive as they have been found nesting nearby in willowherb or even meadowsweet

A BITE IN THE AIR

Sunset brings a special calm to the world of a pond as the activity of day gives way to the unseen moves and sounds of the dark. But between the two lies a twilight zone of half light and dark impenetrable shadows. It is a fascinating time when hunters are out and about, yet at times made almost unbearable by summer swarms of insects. The midge is one of the smallest, more often seen than felt, as the mating dance of the males swarming in the dusk is a predictable part of warm nights over the pond, yet neither sex will bite. Only a little larger another insect is better known as a biter and transmitter of disease in the tropics, where the relationship between mosquito and man is more a state of war. But it's in the short summers of the colder north that mosquitoes mass in their millions. Only the female is a blood sucker as she needs such a meal before laying her eggs, and her mouthparts form a long thin tube adapted for piercing skin. The male is quite different and harmless, feeding only on nectar, so man's problems with mosquitoes are all female.

cling to the empty skin for perhaps several hours. A fall while still soft could cause irreparable damage.

The nymph's body swings from side to side, perhaps checking for clearance before emergence begins, and then it apparently rests. The body pulsates as blood is pumped into the area behind its neck and the rising pressure suddenly ruptures the skin. Revealed inside, a bright green colour becomes increasingly evident with every rhythmical pulse as the creature within gradually eases its way out. The struggle and pressure, contractions and extensions eventually come together and a strange, tender, green body pulls first its head, and then its legs, clear. Intricately done and almost painfully slow, its abdomen remains inside the skin case as the dragonfly arches back until hanging head down.

Another rest lasts for several minutes before a sudden twitch, and its frail-looking legs reach out as its head jerks up. Grasping its old skin case and at the same time pulling its long body up and out, the insect is free to hang, gleaming and new. The wings are small and crumpled at first, but as blood is pumped into tiny veins they unfurl and begin to grow. Steadily all four wings elongate and flatten. As the hours pass the insect progressively hardens and darkens, though it will be several days before it reaches its eventual bright colour.

The first pale light of day finds the dragonfly waiting on the stem, its case now still clinging on below, and but a shadow of its former self. Glinting in the sun the wings catch the light and quiver in the warmth before, without warning, the dragonfly takes to the air – a creature born to fly.

The emergence of these insects each season is a sequence of events virtually unchanged since their first appearance over primeval swamps – before the days of the dinosaur. For some 300 million years the dragonfly has hawked and darted across ponds, both naturally formed and manmade.

A close relative of the fast flying dragonflies are the more delicate damselflies, with their weaker fluttering flight. Taking less time to transform from underwater nymph to free flying adult, they emerge in early morning. Both damsel- and dragonflies are extraordinary and complex creatures, living

Motionless the predatory early life of the dragonfly waits for passing prey. Tadpoles and even other larvae may be taken with lightning speed by an extendible mask which considerably increases its reach

Living up to its name the young, newly-hatched coot is indeed quite bald. But within a few hours it will be up and out paddling through the pond-side vegetation in search of food with the rest of its family

completely dual lives, one in the water and the other breathing air. Their transformation retraces each season the evolutionary path taken by some animals in the past, from aquatic life to living on the land. Dragonflies are broadly divided into two main groups – the short-bodied darters and the hawkers, large and robust. The names refer to their differing habits; one hawking in a regular path takes insects on the wing; the other, darting out from a favoured perch, seizes its prey before returning to eat.

In a good year the adults may fly for several weeks; in a bad for only a few days. Yet, within their brief aerial lives, mating and egg laying take place. The female of both the damselflies and the hawkers deposits her eggs in a water-plant stem by cutting a slit with the ovipositor and inserting it within. But the darter does not lay her eggs with the care of the hawker; she just drops each one as she dips while hovering the surface. Sinking to the bottom, the eggs hatch in the fine silt layer where the nymphs then stay for most of their predatory lives, for even the hunter can become hunted.

Few fish, if any, are found in small shallow ponds, but annual flooding or stream-fed waters may bring in a few. The three-spined stickleback is a ubiquitous fish of ponds and ditches, small streams and slow running rivers. In winter they gather in familiar tiddler shoals while in summer they tend to go their own watery way. Each male stickleback chooses and defends his own little patch, a territory to be held against fellow intruders. From the dull coloration of the colder months to the breeding hues of spring – bright blue eyes, red underside and mouth – all are set off by fine silvery scales along the back.

Sucking and blowing at the silt, the male stickleback builds a narrow trench which he then covers with a roof of weed stuck together by a mucus secreted from his kidneys. A shelter constructed over the trench completes the stickleback's nest and all that remains is to entice an egg-swollen female into his den. Indeed several may eventually lay up to a hundred eggs at a time. He then follows her through the tunnel and fertilises the spawn.

From then on, care of the eggs and young are the responsibility of the male. Patrolling his territorial patch, he occasionally fans the entrance to the nest to improve the flow of fresh water and the consequent oxygen supply. After nine days the eggs begin to hatch, and the male carefully opens up the nursery nest while continuing to guard his offspring. Any young fish that stray are caught on his paternal patrol, sucked in and spat back into the brood. Potential predators are chased off, and even innocent species may be persistently attacked. After ten more days the young fish, having used up their attached yolk sacs have grown sufficiently to start to stray from the nest. The male gradually loses his colour, as well as his interest in the

A large and unlikely pond predator the buzzard will take a wide variety of prey, especially early in the year when frogs feature in some of their diets as not all buzzards have learnt to exploit this annual early food supply

BIRDS OF A FEATHER

The ability to hatch from an egg and leave the nest soon after entering the world, is shared by many waterbirds. Moorhens and coots, rails and little grebes all produce very advanced young. Strong little legs and a thick covering of down equip these chicks to survive. But while swans and grebes give regular rides to their young as they swim, the carrying of young in the air is relatively rare. There are however reliable reports of both moorhen and water rail flying with a chick clasped up between its parent's feet.

On a still summer's evening a nest full of chicks was seen where earlier only a coot and seven eggs lay. First light next morning brought me back to find one egg still unhatched. From a hole in its side a beak tip moved but the once protective membrane within the shell had dried to form a trap. By gently enlarging the hole, and shading the nest with a bush hat propped on a stick, the chick struggled to get free. Then the peeping of a gyrating, swimming chick around my thigh high waders signalled the rest of the brood's return. A lucky break for the last hatched egg of a coot.

wandering brood which soon disperses through the pond.

Towering above the shallows, the pokerlike parts of the reedmace are, in fact, its flowers, and on a clear summer's day the only clouds around are of pollen released to the wind. More commonly known as bulrush, the plant's linear outlines are broken only by other flowers of the season: pale blue water-forget-me-nots and lilac water plantain, violets and white water lilies.

Passing weeks with little sign of rain have seen the pond steadily shrinking, revealing more of its muddy margins. Tiny pond flies engage in their strange summer dance; the males with their white-tipped wings take the lead, flitting back and forth amongst the mud paddling swarm. White butterflies imbibe vital moisture along with dissolved minerals, and flutter with the pond flies over the same damp ground.

The drying rays of the sun draining the life of the pond perhaps herald its future fate as more land is reclaimed. Hanging from a stem, an ageing dragonfly lies at rest, wings tattered and torn; its seeds of life sown for another generation, it just lingers by the remaining pool, surrounded by the crazy patterns of the drought. The area of drying mud grows as the remaining moisture shrinks day by day. A few tadpoles not yet fully grown struggle in the fast-evaporating warm water. But the majority, metamorphosis complete, are leaving the pond. Hiding around the edges or seeking the shelter of widening mud cracks, they are safe from dessication while watching for tiny flies.

The wildlife of pools such as these, which dry out every few years, manages to survive the ebbing tide of the drought in a variety of ways. Adult insects, such as diving water beetles and whirlygigs, backswimmers and pond skaters can fly away. Frogs and toads migrate, but any fish will die, though any eggs laid in the mud could well survive. Some smaller creatures, such as crustaceans and worms, can even endure dryness in a dessicated condition and exposed fully to the air. But by digging into the mud where a

Opposite: Poised for its first flight a four-spotted chaser dragonfly rests above the dried-out skin of its former self. The white threads are the linings to the air tubes pulled free as the adult emerged

degree of moisture remains, snails and other species are enabled to live on while the surface dries out.

A change in the wind and gathering clouds offer a promise of rain. It is rare for parts of Britain to suffer prolonged periods of fine dry weather, yet when the rain comes at last it is as welcome as in any desert. Despite the darkened sky and distant rumbling thunder, the first few hesitant drops on dried cracked mud appear as a sudden surprise.

A gust of wind blows eddying dust across the remains of the pool, and the reedmace bends with shaking leaves as clouds burst overhead. The sound of pattering rain sends miniature torrents streaming over the earth and the lifeblood that is the pond is renewed once more.

8 A NEW COUNTRY

Day dawns late in December; a cold fresh morning still damp from the showers that passed in the night. A solitary crow calls overhead and the sound of cattle mingles with a rural voice that whistles and urges the dairy herd on down between high banked hedges.

Drifting on the wind is the roar of distant machinery, straining and pulling the ground and tearing a small world apart. An excavator bucket crashes into the earth and drags more of a hedgerow away. In a single scoop it lifts half a day's work for a man and his shovel. Within a few days, two fields have become one, and all that remains of a once thriving hedge is a dark brown scar bordered by green.

It was an old hedge, bursting with growth in the spring – hazel and oak, a holly, field maple and blackthorn, hawthorn, elm, elder, ash and a rose – all in a thirty pace stretch. Assuming the estimated age to be that of a century for each shrub or tree, the hedgerow was indeed of ancient origin, a legacy of some remote age that had survived to the present day. From perhaps before the writings of Domesday for more than a thousand years, that hedge, once part of a wood, had stood the passing and changes of time. Through war and famine, plague and peace, people had farmed the surrounding land, tending and protecting their hedge.

Yet beyond the now-enlarged field a plume of smoke marks more of Man's activity, but this time he is burning the waste from a more constructive labour. While one hedgerow was being destroyed, another was having its existence reinforced. Cutting and laying is an ancient art as old as the hedgerow itself. Following centuries of local tradition, the technique adds strength to the living structure and gives it a new lease of life. Where one man destroys, another man builds, and that has been the way of the world for millenia.

It is thought that the greatest achievement of our ancestors with a small population and primitive tools was probably the transformation of a country covered in trees. A primeval forest made into farmland, over a period of some 3,000 years. Today more than eight tenths of Britain is farmed, providing food and a living not only for millions of people, but for a large part of the country's wild animals and plants. What is perhaps even more remarkable is that, having survived for some 150 human generations, the wildlife should be under so much threat from just the last two.

163

BLOCK BUSTING BIRDS

Wildlife sometimes seems incredibly sensitive to disturbance, yet at other times has the ability to survive against overwhelming odds. Many have found man's activities to their advantage seeming to thrive where others apparently fail. On the outskirts of a small Devon village a development had begun of a new housing estate. An old wall enclosed most of the site and at the far end away from the bulldozers and builders, a spotted flycatcher was lining a nesthole protected by wall climbing ivy. As the work of the site grew closer over the following few days the birds deserted to begin building elsewhere.

The noise of trucks and the movement of cement mixers rose in the morning and only went quiet at night. But in the middle of that site surrounded by constant commotion a nest with young birds was discovered. Beneath a mountain of concrete block, a pied wagtail had made a temporary home. Despite men working all round and constantly reducing the pile the bird's entry and exit was never seen. But far from being endangered the workman refused to go near, and the site foreman ordered a new load delivered so that the chicks could fledge in peace.

Down through the centuries Man has changed the course of Britain's natural history, and will no doubt continue to do so in the forseeable future. At a casual glance one may be forgiven for mistaking grassland for a wild meadow or a few trees for native wood, but the superficial resemblance sometimes goes far beyond that. Yet modern machinery is not entirely to blame for the disappearance or decline of so many wild species. It was, after all, the coming of the Iron Age with its more efficient plough that was the turning point, rather than today's tractors and equipment. Agricultural technology just does a more efficient job in a fraction of the time. The use of power is as much a strength of human achievement as its misuse is a failing, but down on the farm it is the wildlife that suffers the consequences.

The pace of change has seen many a traditional farm swallowed by big business and in the seventeen years from the end of the last world war to 1963, some 85,000 miles of hedgerow were cleared from the countryside of England and Wales – 3 miles out of every 20. Since that heyday of hedge removal the rate has slowed to around 2,000 miles a year and on some farms new hedgerows have even been planted, an event perhaps seen for the first time this century.

Yet so much apparent destruction is not done entirely with mindless motive. Where a hedge has outlived its useful life and even obstructs new farm machinery, grubbing out is a practical necessity rather than something done in spite. The costs were once offset by agricultural aid in the form of government grants; many a hedgerow might still be standing if the money involved had had to come from the landowner's pocket. Subsidies are still available for a wide variety of farmland development, from land drainage to the removal of old orchards. With a large proportion of the more economical agricultural improvements already made, perhaps the future for the remaining acres does not look so bleak.

Opposite: The kestrel is today common and widespread across the country having recovered from a decline in the late 1950s due to chemical poisoning. As a predator at the end of a food chain it was vulnerable to a build up of persistent pesticides

The woodlarks mellow song pouring down from above rolling grassy slopes is not so often heard today. Once to be found across England and Wales its number have declined with agricultural change and a series of severe winters since the middle of this century

Providing that effective management bears in mind the needs of Nature, farming and wildlife are not necessarily incompatible. Farmers earn their living from the soil and as such are an undeniable part of the country; it was, after all, their ancestors who created the farmscape of today. Many have more than a vested interest in the land; countrymen born and bred they also want to see it survive relatively intact. As it was left to them by a previous generation so, too, they can pass it to another; yet they also have the right to a better quality of life. The real danger is of a countryside that, on the surface, appears to retain its inherent character, but which in reality supports an impoverished wildlife.

Chemical control of weeds and pests can undoubtedly have far reaching effects when widely used on the land. Whether they are insecticides to protect the crops or herbicides to kill off competition from other plants, all are lethal. Some are more specific than others and a few are long lasting. There are those designed to eliminate just one particular pest and there are more complex compounds that combine the destruction of weeds with the annihilation of insect populations. Even more disastrous for the surrounding area is when applications go wide of the mark and drifting spray falls beyond the field onto wild vegetation. As this is uneconomic and costly, technology is attempting to place the chemicals only where and when needed.

166

The spectre of persistent pesticides lingers in some parts of the country – the fatal, far reaching and longlasting consequences of the widespread use in the 1960s of DDT and its like. Perhaps surprisingly, there are other equally powerful toxins which are not manmade. The leakage of silage liquor from storage clamps into ponds, rivers and streams can cause great loss of life, as the run-off is up to a thousand times more potent than liquid manure.

Natural events also take their toll. The character of the English countryside in some districts changed radically in the 1970s after the ravages of Dutch elm disease. Millions of trees in woodlands and hedgerows, roadsides, gardens and parks died. The first sign of the disaster came with a curious browning of the leaves at the ends of the tallest branches. The following spring, while other trees burst into leaf, growing their cloaks of green, the elms stayed bare. And what the fungal disease carried by a tiny beetle had begun, the landowner finished by cutting down the dead trunks.

The tenacity and resilience of wildlife, to survive and even thrive in the face of adversity, is the strength of Nature itself, as nowhere is devoid of life. In every odd corner and undisturbed building, and from the farmhouse to the field, each species has found a niche. But they are not isolated individuals, self supporting and living alone; they are all part of a larger wild community dependent in some way on each other. When the pressures

Old, undisturbed, damp meadows are traditionally the place for cowslips to be found, but anywhere the conditions are suitable these now rare plants can thrive, on motorway or roadside verge and even in a churchyard

The peace and tranquility of a Devon valley appears only to alter with the gradual progression of the seasons. An annual cycle of growth and decay dictated by the pattern of the weather.

January snow   May grass cutting

become too great, the cracks begin to show.

In sharp silhouette against grey skies, a flock of rooks explodes from the topmost branches of an isolated oak, their receding calls echoing their decline. As a possible indicator of change and as a measure of past and present pressure, the population of rooks has steadily decreased over the past few decades. A study of nesting surveys revealed that the numbers of these familiar black birds, which feed on and make use of almost every feature of the farm, had virtually been halved in many parts of the country. The barn owl, too, is another bird that has disappeared from former haunts especially in the last few years, and for reasons that are not entirely clear. Whether it is a symptom of the times or a longer term cycle, the decline of one species may be just the visible effect of another more serious problem. Only in recent years has the cause for concern been sufficient for national policies positively to begin protecting from themselves the environment that people live in. And that benefits wildlife too. The setting up of reserves, advisory groups, the publicising and making of awards to farms for practical conservation, is no doubt a pointer to future trends. But any major changes in Nature-protecting policies can only be brought about by the will of the majority in a democratic country.

Large scale changes, however, do occur naturally, having been a fact of life affecting millions of animals and plants over as many centuries. In the past, the world has seen arctic tundra overtaken by forest, and trees giving way to grassland. Long term cycles of polar advance and retreat; rivers drying up

168

Yet in the countryside as a whole there are other more permanent changes that may never return as the course of progress takes new turns

August before the second cut for silage

November and the first frost

and glaciers changing course; savannahs becoming desert and lakes becoming land, have all taken place over years usually counted in millenia.

Adapting to change has been one of the driving forces behind the pace of evolution. With the coming of mankind, his moving into the heavens and shifting vast quantities of earth, the world has witnessed changes of awesome proportions – the transforming of entire landscapes in a matter of days and the destruction of natural food chains at a stroke. The interdependence of life from the simplest plant to the most successful predator, is not fully understood. And with over two million different species of living organisms worldwide, the relative importance of one compared to another can be hard to define.

Even on a traditional farm, the range and variety of stock and crop owe their existence and origin to the wild. Jungle fowl from the forests of India have changed remarkably little over their years of domesticated life, yet new varieties are continually being bred – Charles Darwin named thirteen principal types of poultry and modern breeders today list well over a hundred.

Cattle have come from across Europe in addition to many different shapes and sizes of sheep and pig; goats from the Middle East and Asia and the horse of pan-Eurasian breed. The New World contribution to the farmyard zoo came in the form of the weird and wonderful North American turkey, renowned for its curious call. Domesticated ducks descend from wild mallard which has an almost global distribution along with the goose.

169

Combined with the growth of cereal and root crops, fruit and vegetables, the modern farm is as much a product of Man's ingenuity and travel as it is of natural selection, the evolution of life. To benefit the human race whatever else awaits to be discovered, only time and its continuation will tell.

Increasing human populations make greater and stronger demands on a country's resources. Just as Britain's first farmers began to shape a new landscape with no preconceived plan for the centuries ahead, so their descendants at times seem to continue the change. The difference today is the vast increase in knowledge of life, enriched by past practical experience of both disasters and gains, that should enable a future to be planned.

Simply to maintain outmoded traditions while clinging to nostalgic images of the past may not necessarily be the best way forward in the interests of Nature and Man. But a better understanding and awareness of the needs for natural life today make ignorance no excuse. To deny a nation its heritage is to deny a future for mankind.

An everchanging story and dramatic sequel to the emergence of Britain as an island has seen a country reshaped. In parts stripped naked, in others replanted, yet somewhere retaining the elements of its native character. A far cry from primeval pools and ancient forests, the landscape today is a living reminder of our own history on the land, and the wildlife that survives is far more than just a chapter in the secret nature of the countryside.

Opposite: Red squirrels were once to be found across much of Britain but a marked decline around the turn of the century made them rare in the south. It was not however a man-made turn of events as a natural disaster is thought to have wiped them out

9 A GUIDE TO THE COUNTRYSIDE AND WILDLIFE WALKS

The wildlife of the British Isles is rich and varied reflecting the nature of the underlying land as much as the height of the hills and the prevailing climate. This is a guide to the countryside of rural Britain, rather than the wilderness areas. Of native, deciduous woodlands, freshwater pools, farms and open grassland, a taste of the countryside explored in this *Secret Nature*.

Each of the sites are listed under the relevant county and accompanied by an Ordnance Survey national grid number. All are open to the public and more information can usually be obtained from the listed management authority or trust.

ENGLAND

Avon and Somerset

Biddle Combe Nature Trail
Wells Natural History and Archaeological Society
Passing through grassland, woodland and along-side a stream it's a good opportunity to see a range of lime-loving species, some on damp ground.
ST 569488

Brockley Combe Nature Trail
Avon Wildlife Trust
The walk runs through a woodland valley with native trees on limestone and a variety of typical birds.
ST 483663

Bromfield Walk
Somerset Trust for Nature Conservation
This trail passes through farmland, woods and plantation forest, and also offers fine views over Somerset and across the Severn into Wales from the edge of the Quantock Hills.
ST 222322

Five Pond Wood Trail
National Trust and Somerset Trust for Nature Conservation
Running along a streamside, woodland walks in the spring are spectacular with bluebells under the trees and marsh marigolds at the streams edge.
ST 223321

Horner Wood
National Trust
An ancient woodland on the edge of Exmoor, with a wide variety of plants and animals living amongst tall trees and once coppiced wood. The streams attract a good bird life while the forest offers a chance to see pied flycatcher, redstart and wood warbler. Red deer are also resident especially in winter.
SS 897454

Hurscombe
Somerset Trust for Nature Conservation
A reserve containing old farmland gradually giving way to returning scrub, set below the Brendon Hills. Wetland areas also run alongside the reservoir which attracts some wintering ducks.
SS 94317

Weston Woods Nature Trail
Woodspring District Council
A mainly planted woodland with a variety of birds and butterflies in a reserve not far from Weston-super-Mare.
ST 327627

172

Bedfordshire and Huntingdonshire

Aversley Wood
Woodland Trust
A large, and in parts, ancient woodland with spectacular spring flowers, and a wide variety of native trees. A feature is the black hairstreak butterfly found around the thickets of blackthorn.
TL 160817

Flitwick Moor
Bedfordshire and Huntingdonshire Naturalists Trust
An interesting reserve of meadow and woodland. Flooded in the aftermath of the Roman withdrawal, the area became a fen. Falling water levels have since returned the moor to grazing land and wood. A place rich in wild species where over ninety different birds have been counted. Some wetland areas still remain, adding to the diversity of plants and animals to be found.
TL 046354

King's Wood
Bedfordshire County Council
A mixture of old grassland and ancient wood supporting a wide range of plants. From meadow to trees the birdlife is typical of the area.
TL 037393

The Lodge
Royal Society for the Protection of Birds
An area of woodland and heath around the RSPB headquarters, not open on Sundays except to members. Woodland wildlife is typical and the number of species has been increased by careful management and the construction of a lake. A hide overlooks this area and another is situated not far away on Jack's pond.
TL 188478

Totternhoe Knolls
Bedfordshire and Huntingdonshire Naturalists Trust/Bedfordshire County Council
Surmounted by the site of a Norman castle this reserve shows many features of change at the hand of man. Once well wooded the trees gave way to grazing pasture before being replanted. Both stone and lime were quarried in the past but today the reserve contains stands of beech and grasslands rich in wild flowers and butterflies.
SP 986216

Berkshire

Englemere Pond Nature Trail
Bracknell District Council
A dense reedbed offers a chance to see different waterbirds as well as those attracted by the rich insect life of the area. Wetlands and woodlands also fringe the pond.
SU 902684

Thatcham Reedbeds
Newbury District Council
One of the largest reedbeds in this part of the country it attracts good numbers of migrant birds early and late in the year. Wildfowl, waterbirds and warblers are all common, with over fifty different bird species recorded. Wetland flowers and interesting insect life also feature on the reserve.
SU 501673

Windsor Great Park
Crown Estate Commissioners
An ancient hunting forest with many beautifully mature trees. One near the entrance is thought to be around eight hundred years old. A fascinating link with Norman Britain, the entire park is rich in woodland, water and heathland species. From deer to ducks, badgers and butterflies, the history and nature of this royal park is fascinating. It contains one of the finest surviving original oak and beech woods in Britain and also includes coppice and conifers adding to the richness of its wildlife.
SU 953735

Buckinghamshire

Black Park Nature Trail
Buckinghamshire County Council
The walk passes through deciduous woodland and coniferous plantation. The waterside trail also adds to the diversity of the wildlife, showing the contrast in plants and animals to be found in different surroundings.
TQ 005833

Church Wood
Royal Society for the Protection of Birds
A pond has been added to this reserve containing woodland and grass with scrub. Rich in wild birds some eighty species have been counted during the year, over half of which have been recorded as nesting. A wealth of butterflies and flowers, woodland mammals and waterbirds make up a varied wildlife.
SU 973873

Ivinghoe Beacon
National Trust
A range of grassland hills is a popular visitor attraction supporting a rich variety of chalkland butterflies and flowers. The birdlife is also good and alongside the paths there are some spectacular displays of orchids.
SP 961168

Cambridgeshire

Buff Wood
University Botanic Gardens
Only the north west part of this reserve is open

but it is a good opportunity to see some woodland where coppicing has cleared the canopy and encouraged a rich display of flowers. Noted for its hybrids between oxslip and primrose, hellebore also grows amongst the oak, ash and hazel.
TL 283509

Coe Fen and Paradise
Cambridge City Council
With a colourful fringe of streamside plants this reserve is mainly an area of grazing land. The birdlife is enhanced by the variety of insects and flowers.
TL 448575

Devil's Dyke
Cambient/Cambridgeshire County Council
An ancient earthwork well known for its spring flowers many of which can no longer be found in the surrounding countryside, long since lost to the plough. But far from being just a straight raised grassy track, there are parts densely covered in scrub affording cover for birds.
TL 570660-654585

Wandlebury
Cambridge Preservation Society
An interesting country park with an Iron Age fort has been planted with a range of trees. Some chalkland grass still remains and a number of birds breed every year.
TL 493533

Wicken Fen
National Trust
A rich fenland reserve offering many different walks along waterways and between the trees. A good place for watching a range of wild birds from drumming snipe to warblers, wildfowl and even woodcock. Views across the wetlands can be seen from the Tower hide and the visitor centre provides plenty of details about the natural and human history of the site.
TL 563705

Cheshire

Dibbinsdale
Wirral Borough Council
Containing a possible woodland relic from the last Ice Age this area also includes open areas of grass, parkland, reedbeds and meadow. A rich insect life and variety of birds are one of the reserves main features.
SJ 345827

Lyme Park Country Park
National Trust/Stockport Metropolitan Borough Council
A large parkland with a number of fine mature trees is best known for its herd of red deer.
SJ 966842

Marbury Country Park
Cheshire County Council
Woodland walks and a hide overlooking Budworth mere and the Marbury reedbeds provide the visitor with a chance to see a wide range of wildlife. The park also contains the headquarters of the Cheshire Conservation Trust.
SJ 651763

Styal Country Park
National Trust
Passing through the Bollin valley the walk passes riverside and woodland wildlife, rich in birds and mammals.
SJ 835830

Tatton Park Country Park
Cheshire County Council
The forester's walk guides the visitor around a wetland with a variety of birds, and includes well-wooded areas and scrub.
SJ 745816

Cornwall and the Isles of Scilly

Chysauster
Not far from Penzance the remains of this Iron Age village bear witness to the antiquity of settlements in the area, dating from just over two thousand years ago. Small fields and once cultivated plots surround the still standing stone walls built by Celtic farmers.
SW 460355

Coombe Valley Nature Trail
Cornwall Trust for Nature Conservation
Walking along this woodland trail with planted conifers and native trees there is always a chance to see something of interest, particularly in the plants such as autumn crocus and winter heliotrope. Along the waterside there are also dippers and even the occasional flash of a kingfisher colour.
SX 423681

Cotehele Nature Walk
National Trust
Set in the grounds of a beautiful old country estate on the western edge of the Tamar the walk passes through a riverside wood and overlooks an area of marshland.
SX 423681

Isles of Scilly
Duchy of Cornwall/Nature Conservancy Council
Some of the most remote inhabited islands in Britain have a beauty that almost defies description. Tiny sheltered fields contain a unique selection of wild flowers while the remains of prehistoric buildings lie scattered along the coast. Seabirds and spectacular scenery form a magnificent backdrop to a fascinating natural history.

Lanhydrock Nature Walks
National Trust
Reaching up either side of the River Fowey the woodland contains a wealth of wildlife to be found along an attractive walk.
SX 099635

The Lizard
Nature Conservancy Council/Cornwall Trust for Nature Conservation
The diverse nature of the peninsula is a result of its complex geology and a mild climate tempered by warm south westerly winds. A combination of downlands, wet and dry heath, coastal and cliff lands support a wide range of plants and animals. The fields beyond show all the signs of an ancient Celtic origin.
SW 701140

Tregassick Nature Walk
National Trust
Beginning at Percuil the walk winds its way along the riverside and ends at the farm not far from another interesting walk from St Anthony-in-Roselands, which passes through woods and farmland.
SW 857340

Cumbria

Arnside Knot Nature Walk
Arnside Parish Council/National Trust
Set in limestone country the trail passes through typical woodland with a rich range of wildlife including the native red squirrel.
SD 451773

Friars Crag Nature Walk
National Trust
Along the lake edge of Derwent water, circling the shore, a woodland walk gives a view of lakeland wildlife.
NT 264227

Loughrigg Fell Nature Walk
National Trust
Passing along and over the river, through woodland, farmland and upland fell, the circular trail begins and ends at Ambleside.
NY 375047

White Moss Common Nature Walk
National Trust
The beauty of Cumbrian lakes, woodland, fell and farmland is the essence of this countryside along with its bird and plant life.
NY 348065

Derbyshire

Buxton Country Park
Buxton and District Civic Association
Deciduous woodland and Poole's Cavern are the main attractions of this park, with clearings and meadows where upland plants can be found, such as the mountain pansy.
SK 050727

Elvaston Castle Country Park Nature Trail
Derbyshire County Council
A wooded and wetland trail leads through clearings where spring flowers bloom. The birdlife is typical of oak, birch and ash trees while the lake and stream attract many waterbirds.
SK 413332

Hardwick Park Nature Walk
National Trust
Passing ponds and parkland the plant and animal life is seen from a circular trail.
SK 453640

Longshaw Nature Walks
National Trust
A variety of different length walks gives a series of views from open moor to well-wooded valley, past ponds and meadows. The wildlife can be seen in a wide range of habitats as the paths also pass plantations and rough grazing.
SK 267800

Devon

Arlington Court Nature Walk
National Trust
Early in the year a heronry high in the trees is occupied by a number of these impressive birds. The nests overlook a wildfowl sanctuary and also includes a riverside woodland.
SS 611405

Avon Valley Woods
Woodland Trust
Following the Avon valley a steep old oak coppice wood runs along the riverside. Spring flowers and woodland as well as riverside birds can all be seen on the walk.
SX 736509

Bovey Valley Woodlands
Nature Conservancy Council
Keeping to the rights of way a mixed broadleaf wood has a good variety of birds including redstart and wood warbler with pied flycatchers. The river rising on Dartmoor not only adds a damp lushness but attracts dipper and grey wagtail as well.
SX 789801

Chapel Wood
Royal Society for the Protection of Birds
A chance to see buzzard and raven in this mixed oak woodland in early summer, also contains other typical plants and animals.
SS 483415

175

Dunsford Wood
Devon Trust for Nature Conservation
In the upper reaches of the Teign valley the wild daffodils in spring are worth a visit alone. Open woodland with a number of large wood ant colonies and a good selection of butterflies and birds can be seen on the walk.
SX 805883

Heddon Valley Nature Walk
National Trust
The path encompasses a coastal valley passing through mature oak woodland and rich damp meadows.
SX 655483

Lady's Wood
Devon trust for Nature Conservation
This woodland is carefully managed for some fine displays of spring flowers brought about by regular coppicing. Oak and ash trees as 'standards' rise above the cut hazel and ash. Look out for the discarded nutshells from a dormouse's meal, as this reserve is a noted place for these small nocturnal mammals.
SX 687591

The National Shire Horse Centre
Not far from the South Devon village of Yealmpton magnificent shire horses and old country crafts are a major attraction. A working forge and wheelwrights shop as well as displays and parades of horses and wagons are all daily events.
Off A379 Plymouth–Kingsbridge Road.

Welcombe and Marsland Valleys
Royal Society for Nature Conservation
On the border between Devon and Cornwall this reserve contains a rich and varied wildlife with some fine views. From streamside woods to once farmed fields it's an interesting place to see open land being reclaimed by the forest. Butterflies and many badger trails are a feature of the walk as are the wild flowers.
SX 214174

Yarner Wood
Nature Conservancy Council
A series of walks both long and short take you through mainly oak wood. In summer pied flycatchers and redstarts are commonly seen. There are also wayside exhibits and a cabin with plenty of illustrations to help identify the wildlife.
SX 785788

Dorset

Boyden Wood
Woodland Trust
A woodland in the making for this was once open farmland which has been planted with many broad-leaved trees. As it grows so too will the wildlife value of this small wood.
ST 404026

Brounlie Wood
Woodland Trust
This is another young deciduous wood in the making planted in an area that also contains three ponds, adding to the natural diversity of the reserve.
ST 601118

Brownsea Island
Dorset Naturalists Trust/National Trust
Apart from the obvious waterbird life this island is a strong hold for the red squirrel in Southern England. Sika deer and a heronry add to the wildlife list and there are also areas of wet woodland, all to be seen between April and September. No dogs are allowed and access is by boat from Poole Quay or Sandbank Ferry. There are also regular guided walks.
SZ 032877

Green Hill Down
Dorset Naturalists Trust
A chalk downland with scattered stands of oak and ash contains a variety of wildlife habitats, including some beech trees and a small pond. Access is restricted to the bridleways and dogs are not allowed.
ST 792037

Radipole
Royal Society for the Protection of Birds
Reedbeds and open water attract many birds especially spring and autumn migrants. Bearded tits breed regularly amongst the reed.
SY 676796

Durham, Tyne and Wear and Cleveland

Auckland Park Nature Trail
Wear Valley District Council
A parkland trail leads through native and exotic trees with some hawthorn scrub, and a tributary stream to the Wear adds interest to the walk.
NZ 215803

Barnes Park Nature Trail
Sunderland Borough Council
This is another streamside trail through a parkland of mixed trees with a good selection of wild flowers, butterflies and birds.
NZ 383557

Bowlees Visitor Centre
Durham County Conservation Trust
The centre was set up to explain the natural history of the area and the trail leads through ash woodland and uplands with some hawthorn scrub. A spectacular waterfall is a feature which adds to the lushness and different birds.
NY 907283

Castle Eden Dene
Peterlee Development Corporation
A river winds through a deep, well-wooded ravine

A frog's eye view of a fellow amphibian shows some of its adaptations to a half submerged aquatic life — eyes and nostrils on top of its head

carved into the limestone plateau. Spring flowers and broad-leaved trees, red squirrel and roe deer, are just a few of the species found in this wild place to be seen from a walk along one of its tracks.
NZ 410387

Hardwick Hall Country Park
Durham County Council
A walk on raised boards crosses a wetland that was once a lake. Typical birds of wet woodlands are the main feature of this old parkland.
NZ 347292

Rosa Shafto
Durham County Conservation Trust
Spring flowers flood the ground of this mixed woodland. Narrow streams and steep slopes, clearings and dense forest all add to the variety and shape of the country. The bird life is particularly good.
NZ 245350

Swallow Pond
Northumberland Wildlife Trust
Keeping to the rights of way this pond has several different breeding birds and during the seasonal migrations whooper swans and other wintering wildfowl can be seen.
NZ 301693

Washington Waterfowl Park
Wildfowl Trust
Feeding stations bring in an abundance of birds to be seen from hides which overlook the ponds and woods. The visitor centre also includes facilities for the handicapped.
NZ 330565

Essex

Basildon Nature Trail
Basildon Development Corporation
This countryside nature trail passes through woodland and grass, crossed by hedgerows and streams. Small fields and old pasture even derelict gardens all add to the interest along the way.
TQ 715876

Danbury Group
Essex Naturalists Trust/National Trust
A series of circular walks encompasses nine woodland sites. Around the village each has its own name: The Blackwarden, Blakes Wood and Lingwood Common; Pheasanthouse Wood, Poors Piece, Scrub Wood and Danbury Common;

Woodham Walter Common and Birch Wood. For the range of wildlife and richness of habitats these walks are a special attraction.
TL 782044 (Danbury Common)

Epping Forest
Corporation of the City of London
Parts of this ancient forest remain virtually unchanged since neolithic times. A legacy from the prehistoric past that has survived to the present day. The signs of a once worked woodland lie all around, from overgrown pollards to hazel and ash stools. It is still a magnificent wood with a wealth of animal and plant life retaining that strange timeless quality that permeates all great forests.
TQ 412981

Garnetts Wood
Essex County Council
The native small-leaved lime is today almost a rarity but can be seen here in good numbers. This is still a coppiced woodland providing a range of areas from clearings to densely shaded parts. Birds, butterflies and flowers are all to be found especially in and around the sunlit glades.
TL 635815

Hatfield Forest Country Park
National Trust
Once a part of the great Essex forest, the hunting ground of past kings, open parkland was left between coppiced wood and many fine old trees still stand. The nature trail leads from the lake through woods to ancient meadows rich in flowers and anthills.
TL 546199

Little Burstead
Basildon District Council
A countryside trail passes old hedgerow and heath, pollarded oak and a lake. Farmland also features where lapwings can sometimes be seen.
TQ 674931

Gloucestershire

Crickley Hill Country Park
Gloucestershire County Council
The views and variety of oak tree parkland combined with scrub and limestone grassland make this a popular place for visitors. The nature trail points the way to seeing many typical Cotswold plants. The woodland is beech with a few very old trees and some large spreading oaks.
SO 936163

Forest of Dean
Forestry Commission
This area contains several nature reserves and is an important place for wildlife set between England and South Wales. Parts have been forest

for thousands of years and the ages of man have left their mark on the land. From the very first clearings of the neolithic to the forestry planting today, this great and historic area contains a rich wealth and diversity of life.

Nagshead
Royal Society for the Protection of Birds
Part of the Forest of Dean, this woodland reserve contains large mammals as well as many birds, from pied flycatchers to fallow deer.
SO 606080

Rodborough Common
National Trust
The Cotswold downlands are well known for their flowers, and where the plateau gives way to the slopes many interesting species grow. Orchids and pasqueflowers, harebells and wild liquorice to name but a few, attract many insects including marbled white and blue butterflies.
SO 852035

Slimbridge Wildfowl Sanctuary
Wildfowl Trust
Housing the headquarters of the world's largest wildfowl collection the surrounding pools and flooded meadows provide winter grazing for thousands of migrating ducks, geese and swans — an amazing and magnificent sight.
SO 723048

Greater London

Alexandra Park
Haringey Wildlife Group/Alexandra Palace Development Team
At the edge of the old racecourse a mixed range of woods, grassland and a pond give a varied introduction to the nature of this reserve.

Selsdon Wood
National Trust/London Borough of Croydon Reserve
A woodland bird sanctuary and area of grassland where early purple orchids grow make up this reserve. Some coppicing is kept up in parts and a number of interesting birds breed each year.
Court Wood Lane, Selsdon

Thameside
Thameside Association
Founded on the wastelands of an old power station this reserve is a promising site with grasslands, lagoons and dykes. Where skylarks sing overhead an urban farm will help to return the countryside to industrial land.
River Road, Creekmouth, Barking

Upper Wood
Ecological Parks Trust
A range of plants and animals inhabits this once neglected wood of fine mature trees. And the area

is now being managed to enhance its natural value.
Farquar Road, Crystal Palace, SE19

Walthamstow Marsh
Lea Valley Authority
This site of special scientific interest is the last ancient grassland in the Lea Valley with many wetland and meadow plants recorded, along with sedge warblers in the summer and some wildfowl in the winter.

Hampshire and the Isle of Wight

Brook Nature Trail
Isle of Wight Natural History and Archaeological Society
To contrast the difference between the common flowers of farmland and the smaller downland plants this trail takes a circular and interesting path.
SZ 391839

Butser Ancient Farm
Nexus House, Gravel Hill, Hordean
Within the Queen Elizabeth Country Park lies a project unique in British and world archaeology, the working reconstruction of an Iron Age farm dating from around 300 B.C. A glimpse into times past and the origins that began the making of the countryside we know today. Oxen pull ploughs and Celtic fields, sheep and a thatched round house, all add to the atmosphere of this extraordinary place.

Carisbrooke Walk Nature Trail
Isle of Wight Natural History and Archaeological Society
A countryside walk down deep, high-banked lanes. Shady woods and sunlit clearings with a stream show some of the islands life, accompanied by the sound of songbirds in early summer.
SZ 484876

Compton Down
National Trust
A chalk downland with views out to the sea is covered with herbs and grass. Early gentian, cowslips and orchids can all be found, and later the colour of Adonis and Chalkhill blue butterflies, as well as other winged migrants add to the colourful scene. Clouded yellows are attracted by the low growing vetch and even the rare glanville fritillary may be seen.
SX 368854

New Forest
Forestry Commission and others
Once a royal hunting forest the history of this wood reaches even further back in time. Beneath the huge old trees herds of deer still graze in sunlit clearings, and it remains one of the richest places for wildlife, despite the changes wrought over many years by man. A magnificent old and majestic wood with a secret nature to match.

Queen Elizabeth Country Park
Hampshire County Council/Forestry Commission
The centre provides information to explain the natural history to be seen from the walks, a series of trails through woodland and onto the downs.
SU 717186

Selbourne Hill
National Trust
Once the walk of Gilbert White famed for his insight and knowledge on the natural history of the area – a common and beechwood hanger. Coppiced trees and pollarded beech indicate the antiquity of use by people long ago. The variety of trees and rich woodland life, provides a clue to the fascination of the place.
SU 735337

Wellington Country Park
Wellington Enterprises
A series of five walks leads you through woodland, meadows and a lake with great crested grebe. Oak and beech with coniferous plantation are cut by open rides where woodland butterflies are seen.
SU 724626

Hereford and Worcester

Brockhampton Woodland Walks
National Trust
A mixed woodland and lakeside walk is good for a number of birds especially those found around mature oak. The lake adds the interest of some water birds such as the little grebe and wildfowl.
SO 893543

Croft Castle Nature Walks
National Trust
Walks of various lengths pass parkland and avenues of trees while from the limestone scarp views are said to extend over fourteen counties. Buzzards soaring above the slopes and pied flycatchers in the woods are also to be seen.
SO 463655

The Knapp and Papermill
Worcestershire Nature Conservation Trust
Within a relatively small area valley wood, pasture and brook create a rich reserve. Wetland plants and steep wooded slopes where wild service trees and small-leaved lime grow undisturbed. Butterflies and birds along with resident badgers make up the varied fauna list.
SO 748522

Waseley Hills Country Park
Herefordshire and Worcestershire County Council
Bluebells cover the floor of the wood included in

179

the park and a coppice is carefully managed. A marsh and two ponds make up the other areas adding to the nature seen on the walks and explained by the visitor's centre.
SO 979768

Wyre Forest
Nature Conservancy Council
One of the most important wildlife reserves in the Midlands, oak woodland is a key feature and one of its strengths. Bordering the river Severn, this great forest is also one of the few remaining stands of native wood in the country. Centred around the fast-flowing Dowles Brook much of the plant and animal life has survived virtually intact for centuries.
SO 759766

Hertfordshire

Ashridge Nature Walks
Hertfordshire Natural History Society and Field Club/National Trust
A walk through mixed deciduous woodland of oak, ash, birch and beech may bring a chance encounter with the fallow and muntjac deer that graze this land above the vale of Aylesbury.
SP 971131

Northaw Great Wood Country Park
Welwyn and Hatfield District Council
This mixed woodland probably has an ancient origin but few of the original trees have survived. Coppicing and pollarding are still carried out which adds to the range of habitats attracting more birds.
TL 283038

Rye House Marsh
Royal Society for the Protection of Birds
Views of this wetland reserve from the hide allows you to watch a good number of birds. The pools and extensive reedbeds also attract migrants each year.
TL 386100

Tring Reservoirs
Nature Conservancy Council
Although originally man-made the fresh-water life to be seen from the walks is well worth a visit. Apart from an abundance of aquatic plants the public hides give good views of a variety of birds both resident and migrants.
SP 919141

Kent

Blean Wood
Nature Conservancy Council
A well coppiced woodland of ash, and beech, sweet chestnut and hornbeam supports a number of resident birds. As a landfall for many migrants it is also a good place for other birds flying in from the Continent.
TR 118611

Queendown Warren
Kent Trust for Nature Conservation
Once a managed rabbit warren from the time of Henry III the chalk grasslands, scrub and woodlands still supports some rabbits and a wide range of wildlife. Typical downland species and coppiced trees all add to the variety of flowering plants, insects and birds.
TQ 827629

Trosely Country Park
Kent County Council
The forest of beech and hornbeam, oak and ashwood with coppiced stands of hazel surmounts the surrounding escarpment of chalk grasslands and scrub.
TQ 634613

Wye and Crundale Downs
Nature Conservancy Council
Keeping to the rights of way the Downs sweep up from the levels below with views across a patchwork of fields and farms. Created by the first farmers with nibbling flocks of sheep, scrub is now invading as the grazing herds have all but gone. One of the main attractions of this reserve are the orchids that grow in the short dry turf, a sight of exceptional beauty.
TR 077455

Lancashire and Greater Manchester

Alkrington Woods Nature Trail
Rochdale Metropolitan Borough Council
Passing through beech woodland with areas of oak and ash the woodland trail is noted for its range of resident birds.
SD 864053

Astley Park Nature Trail
Chorley Borough Council
The lake attracts an assortment of wildfowl and waterside birds and the woodland path winds

Opposite: A setting sun highlights the shedding of feathery seeds. The bulrush is also known as the reedmace, and is a familiar pond margin plant

between some dense patches of oak and beech with many other trees.
SD 574183

Bramhall Park Nature Trail
Stockport Metropolitan Borough Council
The parkland and lakes are the main attractions with open grassland and woods. A mixed selection of deciduous and conifers bring some interesting birds.
SJ 890863

Cheadle Hulme Nature Trail
Stockport Metropolitan Borough Council
Pasture land and a hedgerow trail attract many small birds and gives a chance to see a species rich old hedge.
SJ 875855

Croxteth Country Park
Merseyside Metropolitan Borough Council
Within this area of farmland and open park over a hundred different birds species have been seen. With ponds and pasture as well as woodlands of many mixed trees it is a place of interest.
SJ 399943

Leighton Moss
Royal Society for the Protection of Birds
Rich in reedbeds, marsh and scrub the Moss is a wonderful reserve for birds but is also good for other plants and animals. Rich in freshwater life from the shallows out to the depths there is always something special to be seen at any time of the year.
SD 478752

Roddlesworth Nature Trail
North Western Water Authority
Passing through woodland and following the streamside trail the range of wildlife from plants to birds is an interesting and varied mix.
SD 665215

Leicestershire and Rutland

Bosworth Park
Leicestershire County Council
This traditional parkland with its lake, stream and small ponds has a fine collection of old trees. Once a seventeenth century deer park, the wetlands are the main attraction for wildlife.
SK 413033

The Outwoods
Charwood Borough Council
With views across the surrounding farmland, fields and hedgerows of the Soar Valley this is a mixed oak and coniferous woodland on high ground.
SK 515159

Rutland Water
Leicestershire and Rutland Trust for Nature Conservation/Anglian Water Authority
England's second largest man-made lake is of national importance for wildfowl. The surrounding area is also not without wildlife interest as many other birds breed during the year in and around the old meadows. Many new woodlands have been planted and that will only add to the value of this already rich site.
SK 897049

Swaithland Woods
Bradgate Park Trust
Much of the wood is ancient with signs that the oaks were once coppiced, but that was probably more than a century ago and the trees have now grown into high forest. Hazel scrub beneath the oak increases the natural value by providing a rich understorey. A woodland stream is another attraction both for the human visitor and the wild.
SK 538129

Lincolnshire and South Humberside

Bradley Woods
Grimsby Borough Council
For a variety of woodland birds the mixed deciduous trees offer food and shelter while in the wet clearings common spotted orchids grow. Badger trails are often seen and butterflies haunt the sunlit glades.
TA 245058

Elsham Hall Country Park Nature Trails
Three trails lead out and around the purpose-built lakes, with plantations, mixed woods and downlands forming an attractive background to the walks.
TA 029120

Snipe Dales
Lincolnshire County Council/Lincolnshire and South Humberside Trust for Nature Conservation
From the way marked route through a narrow neck of woodland and marsh the reserve opens onto a grass valley. Hawthorn scrub with some gorse lie scattered across the slopes. New plantations will add to the attraction of flowering plants while several species of warbler are already known to breed.
RF 320863

Norfolk

Blickling Estate
National Trust
The estate is typical of the larger East Anglian parklands with woods, farmland and a lake. Visiting and resident waterbirds can frequently be seen.
TG 175287

Broadlands Conservation Centre
Norfolk Naturalists Trust
To reach this wetland trail visitors must use the carpark at TM 359146 and from there use the raised walkways passing through wet fen to the floating conservation centre. The man-made origins and wildlife of the broads are all well explained.
TN 356149

Otter Trust
To see an otter in the wild is today a rare and unlikely event so this provides a good opportunity to watch them in semi-natural conditions. A nature trail and wildfowl collection are also added interests.
TM 315884

Ringstead Downs
Norfolk Naturalists Trust
From the track running through the valley the chalk downlands lie on either side, with many typical flowering plants, butterflies and birds.
TF 706400

Strumpshaw Fen
Royal Society for the Protection of Birds
Fen and woodland with extensive areas of grazing marsh are the landscape feature of the reserve. But the life lies in the number of birds found in reedbed and open water. All three native woodpeckers inhabit the woodlands and several wading birds nest out in the meadows. Swallowtail butterflies and even marsh harriers all breed on this reserve.
TG 342067

Northamptonshire and Peterborough

Barnack Hills and Holes
Nature Conservancy Council/Northampton Trust for Nature Conservation
The limestone grassland supports a wonderful spread of flowers typical of such country. The pasqueflower is one of the most important but spring is the time for cowslips. Some fifty species of birds have been recorded within the reserve and the flowers draw in a good number of attractive butterflies.
TF 075046

Castor Hanglands
Nature Conservancy Council
A right of way leads through the reserve of woodland, scrub and grasslands with many wet areas and a stream fed pool. A part of the ancient forest of Narborough, the wood was enclosed and managed for coppiced timber before being clear felled. Grasslands kept by grazing eventually gave way to scrub and now other birds and insects have returned.
TF 118023

Lings Wood
Northampton Trust for Nature Conservation
From the trust's headquarters a nature trail leads out into the reserve of mixed woodland. Coniferous and some deciduous trees make up the majority of the area. Butterflies are well represented with fifteen species so far seen.
SP 802638

Northumberland

Arnold
Northumberland Wildlife Trust
The nature of one of the few semi-natural woodlands and scrub of the area is explained at the visitor's centre. Ash, elm and sycamore with stands of pine are the taller trees while there is also a layer of shrubs. Some interesting birds have been recorded including the icterine warbler and wryneck.
NU 255197

Cragside Country Park
National Trust
Once open moorland the planted park was established with trees and lakes in which a nature trail winds and a visitor's centre is set.
NU 072015

Plessy Woods Country Park
Northumberland County Council
From the visitor's centre a trail leads into the park set on the banks of the River Blyth. A wooded valley where roe deer and red squirrel are found and the dipper that frequents the river.
NZ 238800

Nottinghamshire

Clumber Park
National Trust
Winter is the time to see wildfowl on the lake but through the rest of the year there are other birds and plants to be seen. A former Sherwood forest estate now has a visitor's centre and nature trail.
SK 645773

Martin's Pond
Nottingham City Council/Nottinghamshire Trust for Nature Conservation
Within 1.5km of the city boundary over seventy bird species have been recorded, and of those some twenty-four are known to have bred. A path encircles the pond and a walkway gives access and an unusually interesting view of the reeds with its waterbirds and warblers.
SK 526402

Sherwood Forest Country Park
Nottingham County Council
A large woodland that is but a small part of ancient Sherwood Forest. A place where old oaks

grow with stands of birch and bracken and also good for a wide range of woodland life.
SK 627677

Oxfordshire

Aston Rowant
Nature Conservancy Council
Set on steep chalk slopes the varied Chiltern scarplands give rise to open grass, scrub and beechwood with some spectacular views across the countryside. From the visitor's centre the same view is enjoyed and an appreciation of how much chalk grass has disappeared under the plough. Chalkland butterflies and flowers are common while much of the bird life can be found around the scrub.
SP 741967

Manor Farm
Cogges, Oxford
The workings of an old Edwardian farm are housed in and around a range of Cotswold stone buildings. Ancient fields and a deserted village are part of the history trail. Some old livestock breeds are also kept on the farm.
SP 370095

Ridgeway Path
A long-distance way following most of the line of chalk hills gives a memorable impression of the richness of countryside wildlife.
SU 259833–SP 770013

Warburg
Berkshire, Buckinghamshire and Oxfordshire Naturalists Trust
In the chalk valley of Bix Bottom lies a wooded reserve where rides and old meadows, clearings and banks create a rich reservoir of natural life. Beech trees stands and hazel coppice hide breeding birds and mammals.
SU 720880

Shropshire

Colemere Country Park
Shropshire County Council
A legacy from the end of the last Ice Age that left a series of shallow waters. Woodland and grassy meadows make up the rest of the reserve which has a good bird and insect life.
SJ 434328

Earl's Hill
Shropshire Trust for Nature Conservation
Once an Iron Age hill fort and now a nature reserve the valley woodlands below give way to grassland hill. Rocky outcrops stand over the surrounding farms and trees grow tall and dense lower down the steep-sided slopes. And a wood-

land stream adds yet another dimension to the wildlife seen.
SJ 409048

Market Drayton Nature Trail
Shropshire Trust for Nature Conservation
An interesting trail leads past everything from a river, canal and hedgerow through woodlands and out into farmland, surprisingly close to town.
SJ 684343

Merrington Green Nature Trail
Shropshire Trust for Nature Conservation
To see the process of reversion from grazing land to wood this is a good trail that also passes a number of pools and wetland areas.
SJ 465209

Staffordshire

Deep Hayes Country Park
Staffordshire County Council
Greater butterfly orchids are a major attraction of the reserve that includes a mixed and varied habitat of pools and marsh, meadows and woodlands.
SJ 962535

Manifold Valley
National Trust/Shropshire County Council
The footpath follows the valley course cut by a river that disappears deep under ground below Wetton Mill, only to reappear much further down at the boil-holes of Illam. But that is only in summer when the course runs dry. Meadows and steep grassy banks are where many flowers grow while much of the bird and mammal life keeps to the cover of the woods.
SK 100543

Rough Knipe
Royal Society for the Protection of Birds
A rich reserve in plant and insect life its mature trees are noted for the nests of pied flycatchers and redstarts. A stream where dippers breed also runs through the valley wood.
SK 009534

Suffolk

Bradfield Woods
Suffolk Trust for Nature Conservation
The ancient art of coppicing is still continued today with parts of this woodland cleared every seven years, as it has been from centuries past. Over 350 flowering plants are known from the woods where the continuation of the coppice ensures their survival. A few deer remain as do many amphibians, while evidence of birds is seen and heard everywhere.
TL 935581

Small and agile the harvest mouse has more than a twist to its tail. Its tip is prehensile and is used to secure a precarious hold as it scrambles amongst tall stems (*Photo. Roger Hosking*)

North Warren
Royal Society for the Protection of Birds
Woodland, fen and grass heath make up most of the reserve, with reeds and willow extending the woods into wetlands. As might be expected it is a good place for many smaller birds as well as the occasional bittern or marsh harrier.
TM 455587

Potash Lane Hedge
Suffolk Trust for Nature Conservation
A tiny and unusual reserve dates from the time of the Norman Conquest. An ancient hedgerow containing many tall trees and others that were pollarded.
TL 994404

Wolves Wood
Royal Society for the Protection of Birds
Mature oak and hazel wood is the setting for this nature trail. The number and variety of woodland's birds only being outdone by the insects and flowers. Increasing the size of the glades enlarges woodland edge and that in turn brings in more birds and makes them easier to see.
TM 054436

Surrey

Bookhams Commons Nature Walks
National Trust
The trails of different lengths are set in an area of grassland and wood. Old fish ponds and invading scrub add to the interest and wildlife of the place.
TQ 121567

Horton Country Park
Epsom and Ewell Borough Council
Cut late in the year with no herbicide sprayed or fertilisers 'improving' the grass, the meadows are managed to allow a colourful spread of spring and summer flowers. Woodland birds are also attracted by the various hedgerows and woods.
TQ 191618

North Downs Way
Countryside Commission
From Farnham to Dover in Kent, on the crest of the Downs, gives some spectacular views across farmland.
SU 844467–TQ 429561

Thursley

Nature Conservancy Council
Deciduous forest once covered the heathlands of Surrey until prehistoric people cleared by burning and felling. Farmed and grazed the sandy soils eventually gave way to heath. From the turn of the century the cessation of grazing saw the return of trees, only this time birch and Scots pine. Here the visitor can see the transformation created by man to bog, heathland and wood.
SU 900399

Sussex

Arundel Wildfowl Refuge

Wildfowl Trust
Open water, reeds and wet marshy fields are the ingredients that make this reserve a haven for birds viewed from the hides. Waders and ducks breed and many more are seen on migration especially during the winter months.
TQ 020081

Black Down Nature Trail

National Trust
Mixed woodlands are passed through on this trail which gives magnificent views of the South Downs from the highest point in West Sussex.
SU 921309

Castle Hill

Nature Conservancy Council
Carpets of colour cloak the chalk grasslands where meadow pipits and skylarks sing. Butterflies are an added delight.
TQ 367074

Fore Wood

Royal Society for the Protection of Birds
Growing on an interesting mix of clay and sands the woodlands show many a man-made touch. Stands of sweet chestnut are coppiced, a tree originally imported by the Romans for its edible nuts. Spring flowers and woodland birds are one of the strengths of the reserve.
TQ 756128

Mallydams Wood

Royal Society for the Protection of Cruelty to Animals
A mixture of woodland and heath makes up this mainly educational reserve that typifies many east Sussex woods. Dormice have also been found, some in the nest boxes put up for the birds.
TQ 857122

South Downs Way

Countryside Commission
With views across the chalk cliffs and rolling flower-rich downs the long distance way reaches from the borders of Hampshire to Beachy Head.
SU 762193–TV 600972

Warwickshire and West Midlands

Crackley Wood Nature Trail

Warwick District Council
An oak and birch woodland with a fine display of spring flowers and a number of typical birds.
SP 287737

Draycote Water Country Park

Warwickshire County Council
With a view over the reservoir the hill grassland shows the ancient pattern of a medieval open field system, a ridge-and-furrow ploughing pattern.
SP 467692

Edge Hill Nature Trail

The trail passes through wetland and wood, and grasslands rich in plants and has the added attraction of some spectacular views. The area is also well known for its insects and birds.
SP 370470

Ham Dingle Nature Trail

Dudley Metropolitan Borough Council
Woodland birds and understorey herbs and shrubs are typical with mature stands of oak.
SO 913828

Sandwell Valley Nature Trails

Sandwell Metropolitan Borough Council
Passing through the wooded valley that was once laid out as parkland the trail leads around a number of pools. Woodland and wetland birds are well represented with wintering ducks and waders on passage.
SP 017914

Welcombe Hills Nature Trail

Stratford District Council
The trees attract many woodland birds and the area is well planted with parkland oaks, beech and other mixed species.
SP 205564

Wiltshire

Barbury Castle Country Park

Wiltshire County Council
On the north facing scarp of the Malborough Downs stands Banbury Castle, an Iron Age fortified settlement. With some stunning views across country the area is a fine example of grazed downlands.
SU 157761

Coate Water Country Park

Thamesdown Borough Council
A variety of interesting birds have been recorded from this wetland bird sanctuary, including woodlark and hobby.
SU 178820

North Meadow

Nature Conservancy Council
Old meadow grasslands make up this fine reserve containing a rich and diverse mix of flowers. Cowslips and orchids, oxeye daisy and great burnet, but the plant that makes this such a special place is the rare and attractive fritillary.
SU 099944

Pewsey Downs

Nature Conservancy Council
This magnificent rolling landscape is impressive by any measure. Though grazed for centuries, today most of the sheep have gone, but the turf has retained its colourful flora. These chalk hills were originally formed by the same forces that created the Alps, but cleared of trees and continually close-cropped, producing one of the finest examples of downlands in the country.
SU 115635

Roundway Hill Covert Countryside Trail

Forestry Commission
Passing through mixed woodland a trail circles the slopes planted with stands of beech. The grasslands still contain chalkland plants and there are some fine views of the surrounding country.
SU 005647

Wyle Down

Nature Conservancy Council
Dwarf sedge is rare elsewhere but grows well in the south of the county, along with other plants typical of chalk downlands.
SU 002363

Yorkshire and South Humberside

Fairburn Ings

Royal Society for the Protection of Birds
Subsidence due to mining has created a series of ponds from a former wet area of flood meadows. The autumn migration sees many birds both large and small passing through the reserve. Over one hundred and seventy species are recorded on average each year and up to seventy stay to breed.
SE 460278

Forge Valley Woods

Nature Conservancy Council
A rich wooded reserve with oak on higher ground and a mixed forest below. Woodland birds are common and in spring there is a fine floral display.
SE 985860

Hornsea Mere

Royal Society for the Protection of Birds
Yorkshire's largest freshwater lake attracts many interesting birds and contains a wealth of plant life. Fields and woodland add to the wild attraction.
TA 198473

WALES

Clwyd

Ewloe Castle Nature Trail

Clwyd County Council
Woods and open farmland are the features of the reserve, and the valley through which the trail passes is covered in spring flowers. Small ponds bring in some waterbirds and the plant life is typically wetland around their margins.
SJ 292670

Holywell Nature Trail

Clwyd County Council
Oak, ash and crab apple trees form much of the woodland of the valley, and old industrial ponds provide for waterbirds and aquatic plant life.
SJ 195764

Legacy Nature Trail

Central Electricity Generating Board
The trail passes the remains of man's past activities, demonstrating the colonisation of these areas with natural plant growth. Wetlands and open grass add to the interest with the occasional hunting barn owl.
SJ 295483

Dyfed

Castle Woods and Dynevor Deer Park

West Wales Naturalists Trust
One of the finest woodlands in west Wales overlooking the deer park and wide flood meadows of the valley. A mixed selection of ash and wych elm trees is perhaps all that remains of the original woodland in this part of Wales.
SN 627220

Constitution Hill Nature Trail

West Wales Naturalists Trust/Ceredigion District Council
Grasslands and inland woods with hedge banks create many different places for wildlife to live. And the birds reflect the variety of the surrounding habitat.
SN 583826

Pembroke Upper Mill Pond

West Wales Naturalists Trust
For waterbirds this is an interesting pond which is also the only known Pembrokeshire site for horned pondweed. Winter wildfowl are annual visitors while little grebe have nested.
SM 953161

Penally Nature Trail

Friends of Penally
Set in an area of farmland the countryside trail includes hedgerows and woodland, marsh and grass, and even an ancient cave system.
SS 117991

187

Pengelli Forest
West Wales Naturalists Trust
A once coppiced wood of oak that was once clear felled has an even age of trees. The tall canopy and dense shade shelters an interesting natural history.
SN 124395

Glamorgan

Bute Park Nature Trail
Cardiff City Council
The parkland trail runs along side the River Taff with both native and exotic broad-leaved trees and these attract a typical bird life.
ST 182767

Cefn Onn Nature Trail
Cardiff City Council
Climbing north of Cardiff onto sandstone ground the trail passes woodlands of birch and ash, oak and hazel as well as beech.
ST 184843

Cosmeston Lake Country Park
Water, wood and grassland offer a range of habitats to explore. There is a variety of bird and insect life, and of the plants the orchids are a splendid sight.
ST 180693

Margam Country Park
Several pools and parkland trees are passed by the walks and show the variety of wildlife that includes a herd of fallow deer and a heronry near one of the ponds.
SS 813849

Gwent

Lower Wye Valley
The picturesque views of the valley are flanked by woods and few fields. The woodland is mixed and varies in character along the course of the river. A typical part may contain ash and beech with wych elm and small-leaved lime. Hazel is found lower down and by the water alder grows. It is a fascinating area with an equally interesting natural history.

Offa's Dyke Path
Built to keep the English out of Wales this old defensive dyke supports a path that runs from Prestatyn in Clwyd to Chepstow, passing through some spectacularly beautiful country.
SO 267323–ST 553928

St Mary's Vale Nature Trail
Brecon Beacons National Park Committee/ National Trust
Rising up through the woodlands the steep sided trail is in the foothills of the Sugar Loaf, a towering sandstone hill. Mixed stands of alder and ash with some beech give way to native oak on the other side of the stream.
SO 283162

Gwynedd

Bron-y-Graig Nature Trail
Snowdonia National Park Committee
The walk will take you through some mixed wood, though most is of oak, in parts well overgrown of what was once an old estate.
SH 583311

Coedydd Aber
Nature Conservancy Council
The track that leads up to the magnificent Aber Falls passes through an interesting variety of wood. Oak and hazel with ash, wych elm and birch make up a large part of the walk. Towards the head of the valley and the falls themselves the woodland becomes more open, and then increases as the spray creates a damp dense growth nearby. This wealth of woodland habitat encourages and supports an equally rich wildlife.
SH 662720

Powys

Pwll-y-Wrach
Brenock Naturalists Trust
In the steep valley woods oak grows tall with a rich and varied layer of smaller tree and shrubs. Hazel, hawthorn and holly, even field maple and spindle, all add to woodland life by attracting different species. The river also increases the range of bird life seen, with dippers and wagtails commonly seen.
SO 163327

SCOTLAND

Borders, Dumfries and Galloway

Duns Castle
Scottish Wildlife Trust
Spring flowers cover the floor of this mixed woodland which is dominated with beech and some fine oaks. The bird life is further enhanced by an artificial loch which is also sometimes visited by the otter.
NT 778550

Ken-Dee Marshes
Royal Society for the Protection of Birds
Winding along the valley floor Loch Ken and the River Dee are fringed with waterside plants and flanked by woodland and fields. The wintering grounds for vast flocks of Greenland white-

fronted geese, while in summer there are wet meadows, flowers and woodland birds.
NX 6376 and 6869

Grampian

Crathes
National Trust for Scotland
Set in the grounds of Crathes Castle mature deciduous wood, plantation, a pond and old sand diggings provide an interesting range of habitats for red squirrel and many birds.
NO 7396

Dinnet Oakwood
Nature Conservancy Council
One of the few remaining oak woods in north east Scotland provides a home for many woodland birds.
NO 464980

Drum
National Trust for Scotland
Mature oak and beech with Scots pine are the main features of this old wood providing guided walks in the summer.
NJ 7900

Leith Hall
National Trust for Scotland
Two trails lead through woodland moor and farmland, one passes mainly through mixed plantation the other through native trees and to a pond.
NJ 5429

Islands

Orkney, Shetland and Outer Hebrides
The farming countryside of these islands still maintain many rural crafts no longer seen on the mainland. Haystacks and late cut long-grassed meadows. The Machair of North Uist is included in an RSPB reserve where many wading birds breed.

Strathclyde

Argyll Forest Park
Forestry Commission
Oak dominates the semi-natural areas of deciduous wood while mixed trees make up the rest that survives in some parts of the park.
NN 272034

Brodick Country Park
National Trust for Scotland/ Cunningham District Council
Oak and beech wood are the background to these walks providing some interesting bird watching.
NS 0138

Culzean Country Park
National Trust for Scotland
Woodlands and ponds are the elements offering a varied wildlife habitat to many different species. A visitor's centre is open from April to October.
NS 2310

Tayside

Pass of Killiecrankie
National Trust for Scotland
The woodland gorge contains a mixed selection of trees dominated by oak. Trails from the visitor's centre feature the plant and bird life of the area.
NN 917627

Vane Farm
Royal Society for the Protection of Birds
The farmland included within the reserve is managed for the benefit of birds, and the crops provide good gleaning for autumn arrivals of geese. Open to visitors at the weekends in winter, January to March, the reserve is closed on Fridays during the rest of the year.
NT 1699

BIBLIOGRAPHY

Bunn, D.S., Warburton, A. B. & Wilson, R.D.S., *The Barn Owl* (T & A D Poyser, 1982)

Corbet, G.B. & Southern, H.N., *The Handbook of British Mammals* (Blackwell Scientific Publications, 1977)

Frazer, D., *Reptiles and Amphibians in Britain* (Collins New Naturalist, 1983)

Hawksworth, D.L. (ed), *The Changing Fauna and Flora of Britain* (Academic Press, 1974)

Hoskins, W.G., *The Making of the English Landscape* (Hodder and Stoughton, 1955)

Imms, A.D., *Insect Natural History* (Collins New Naturalist, 1971)

Lever, C., *The Naturalised Animals of the British Isles* (Hutchinson, 1977)

Mabey, R., *The Common Ground* (Hutchinson, 1980)

The Macmillan Guide to Britains Nature Reserves (Macmillan, 1984)

Matthews, L.H., *Mammals in the British Isles* (Collins New Naturalist, 1982)

Mellanby, K., *Farming and Wildlife* (Collins New Naturalist, 1981)

Mellanby, K., *Pesticides and Pollution* (Collins New Naturalist, 1967)

Murton, R.K., *Man and Birds* (Collins New Naturalist, 1971)

Pollard, E., Hooper, M.D. & Moore, N.W., *Hedges* (Collins New Naturalist, 1974)

Rackham, O., *Trees and Woodlands in the British Landscape* (Dent, 1976)

Russel, E.J., *The World of the Soil* (Collins New Naturalist, 1957)

Sparks, J. & Soper, T., *Owls* (David and Charles, 1970)

Stamp, L. D., *Man and the Land* (Collins New Naturalist, 1969)

Tansley, A.G., *Britains Green Mantle* (Allen and Unwin, 1968)

Thompson, G., Coldrey, J. & Bernard, G., *The Pond* (Collins, 1984)

INDEX